EXPORT CREDIT AGENCIES

THE UNSUNG GIANTS OF INTERNATIONAL TRADE AND FINANCE

Delio E. Gianturco

Q

QUORUM BOOKS
Westport, Connecticut • London

Library of Congress Cataloging-in-Publication Data

Gianturco, Delio E., 1940–
    Export credit agencies : the unsung giants of international trade and finance /
    Delio E. Gianturco.
        p. cm.
    Includes bibliographical references and index.
    ISBN 1–56720–429–5 (alk. paper)
        1. Export credit.   2. International trade.   3. International finance.   I. Title.
    HG3753.G48   2001
    332.7'42—dc21   00–062773

British Library Cataloguing in Publication Data is available.

Library of Congress Catalog Card Number: 00–062773
ISBN: 1–56720–429–5

First published in 2001

Quorum Books, 88 Post Road West, Westport, CT 06881
An imprint of Greenwood Publishing Group, Inc.
www.quorumbooks.com

Printed in the United States of America

The paper used in this book complies with the
Permanent Paper Standard issued by the National
Information Standards Organization (Z39.48–1984).

10 9 8 7 6 5 4 3 2 1

Copyright Acknowledgments

The author and publisher gratefully acknowledge permission for use of the following
material:

Organization for Economic Control and Development. *Arrangement on Guidelines for
Officially Supported Export Credits*. Washington, DC: OECD, 1998.

Contents

Preface

This book was written in bits and pieces beginning in 1977. That was the year I started the consulting firm of First Washington Associates (FWA)—self-described from the outset as the only firm in the world specializing in technical assistance for export credit agencies. The information contained herein represents lessons learned over an even longer period—first as an export credit agency (ECA) manager and then as a consultant.

When FWA started, I had just completed fifteen years with the Export-Import Bank of the U.S. (U.S. Eximbank) rising from its clerical ranks in 1963 to the board of directors in 1976. During that time, I learned that very few people outside the ECAs knew what an export credit agency was or what it did. Many otherwise knowledgeable folks thought that the U.S. Eximbank was the same as the World Bank. However, while at the U.S. Eximbank, I found out some of the differences and absorbed all I could about export credit operations—at least about American ECA operations.

It was not until the early 1970s that I discovered that the American ways of export credit were not the only, or even the best, ways of extending export financing. In 1970, I started regularly attending Berne Union and Organization for Economic Control and Development (OECD) meetings where the world's largest and oldest ECAs, almost all from industrial countries, discuss mutual concerns, problems, and possible solutions. Despite all this exposure, however, I remained relatively ignorant about ECAs of developing countries and how they differed from those of industrial countries.

When FWA began operations, I realized for the first time that most ECAs were not large, well-heeled, industrial country organizations. Indeed, I found the opposite: Most were small- to medium-sized, with tight budgets, residing in developing countries in the Caribbean, Latin America, Asia, Africa, Central and Eastern Europe and the former Soviet Union. I saw many similarities but also realized significant differences in their financial environments, economic problems, government policies and constraints, as well as prospects for their activities.

It is with no small measure of pride that I note that over half of the ECAs that have started up since 1977 have been helped by FWA and that almost all of them have done an excellent job of financing their exporters while maintaining their own soundness. These ECAs have done so without subsidy, distortion of trade patterns, adverse effects on the private financial community, or other bad practices. Of course, the credit for this belongs to the founders and managers of these extraordinary institutions who have done so much, starting with so little.

At the time of this writing, in the year 2000, I reflect on the trials and tribulations of working with ECAs and other financial institutions in almost 100 countries with different languages, cultures, traditions and ways of doing business. I marvel that such a diverse world has knitted itself together as well as it has, largely as a result of international commerce and its accompanying benefits.

It is also interesting to note that a consulting firm such as First Washington Associates could only have existed in the last twenty-five years. Before that time, ECAs were really not appropriate for most countries, and the rapid transportation and telecommunications that made FWA a viable operation did not exist at an earlier period.

Finally, I want to mention that the success of FWA and my ability to write a book of this nature were completely dependent upon our full-time staff and the U.S. and non-U.S. consultants who worked with us on overseas assignments down through the years. These Americans, Canadians, Australians, Europeans, Asians, and Latin Americans added incomparably to my understanding of alternative ECA institutions, programs, policies, and procedures.

I believe this to be the only book that looks at ECAs in their broadest policy context as well as their smallest operational details, distinguishing but giving roughly equal treatment to industrial, developing, transitional, and regional ECAs. As a result of this comprehensive treatment, I hope the reader will see both the "trees" and the "forest." I am confident in referring to the world's ECAs as "unsung giants." Their contributions to economic growth and development and their importance to financial sector capabilities and soundness greatly exceed the limited understanding of ECAs by governments, businesses, and the general public. I hope this volume will help to address and resolve that imbalance.

Acknowledgments

I would like to render special acknowledgment to my colleagues at First Washington Associates for all their contributions to this book, especially Albert Hamilton for his editing and updating of contents, Edward Greene for his sound insights, and Barbara Urban for her assistance with logistics. Gratitude and appreciation is also due to the senior managers of export credit agencies around the world who co-operated with my requests for information and provided much of the information contained herein. I want to acknowledge practical suggestions from Lisa, Grace, and Mark. Most importantly, I want to thank my wife Elizabeth for her support, understanding, and encouragement through the years that I worked on this volume.

Unsung Giants

The "unsung giants" of international finance are the world's export credit agencies (ECAs)—highly specialized financial institutions that currently cover about $800 billion of exports each year but rarely receive the attention of the press or of the average citizen.

One out of every eight dollars of world trade is now financed by ECAs. Much of the remaining seven dollars is influenced by what the ECAs do; whether they advocate a restrictive or expansive policy of selling goods to other nations affects exporters' willingness to trade with particular countries and buyers and influences the terms and conditions on which trade is conducted. There are only about 200 ECAs in the world—domiciled in 100 countries—but their contribution to trade and development has been massive and pivotal to the success of globalization and a healthy world economy.

ECA activity far exceeds that of all multilateral development banks (MDBs), such as the World Bank and the Asian Development Bank. ECA loans, guarantees, and insurance are also far greater than the activity of all overseas development agencies (ODAs), such as the U.S. Agency for International Development. Despite this, few people really know about the ECAs and what they do. The ECAs' relative anonymity cannot be blamed on recent arrival on the world scene: They have been around since 1906, roughly twice as long as the MDBs, which have been operating only since the late 1940s.

Lack of knowledge about the ECAs cannot be traced to a lack of importance. The ECAs have helped their countries cement alliances with other nations, develop overseas sources of raw materials, open up new markets for manufactured products, support friendly nations and punish unfriendly countries, develop the manufacture of new products and strategic industries, promote economic growth in poor countries, facilitate foreign direct investment, and increase their own countries' ability to purchase goods from foreign suppliers.[1] First and foremost, however, they have succeeded in increasing domestic employment, raising business sales and profits, and expanding national tax bases by stimulating exports.

What are the ECAs and what do they do? A generally accepted definition of ECA is as follows: (1) a highly specialized bank, insurance company, finance corporation, or dependency of the government, (2) offering loans and/or guarantees, insurance, technical assistance etc., to support exporters, (3) covering both commercial and political risks related to export sales, (4) with the backing or approval of the national government, and (5) dedicated to supporting the nation's exports. Ownership is usually government or mixed, but privately owned ECAs are rapidly becoming more prevalent and dominant. As for what they do, ECAs provide the financing that is essential for export success, financing characterized by the National Association of Manufacturers of the United States as "the lubricant that keeps the export engine operating smoothly; without it, exports and a growing number of jobs are at risk."[2]

ECA financing takes the form of loans, guarantees, insurance, and related technical assistance which are used to support export sales. In order to fund these operations, the world's ECAs obtain monies from both domestic and international sources that are then lent to their nations' exporters. Most importantly of all, perhaps, the ECAs are a repository of information and technical skill, which are used to show exporters and banks how to extend credit to foreign buyers in a sound fashion. The ECAs excel in the techniques of intelligent risk management, which they apply in their own extensions of short-, medium-, or long-term credit. These techniques are picked up, and carried on, by a nation's exporters and banks, regardless of whether the ECA provides financing or other assistance for a particular sale.

In their extensions of credit for international transactions, ECAs stand in a middle position between the exporters and commercial banks (which prefer to keep export credit relatively short term with high interest rates) and MDBs and ODAs (which lend at very long terms with relatively low interest rates and, in some cases, grants). Most ECA credit activity falls into an intermediate range: longer than thirty days but less than five years, with interest rates close to their country's prime rates. ECAs can lend, guarantee, or insure for longer or shorter periods, but such activity represents a minority of their overall credit extensions.

There are two ways in which most exporters use ECAs: (1) directly by making application to the ECA for a loan, guarantee, or insurance, or (2) indirectly through the exporter's commercial bank, which applies to the

ECA for a loan, guarantee, or insurance. The indirect route is often man-dated by an ECA if a loan to an exporter is involved: The ECA generally prefers to have the commercial bank handle the paperwork, administra-tion, and risks involved in making a loan to an exporter. In these cases, the ECA "rediscounts" the commercial bank's loan, lending money to the commercial bank, which passes it on to the exporter. The exporter has the liability to repay the commercial bank, and the commercial bank has the liability to repay the ECA. To the contrary, insurance is usually issued directly to the exporter by the ECA. In return for a premium paid by the exporter, the ECA insurance covers the risk of nonpayment by the exporter's foreign buyers. If nonpayment from the buyer occurs, the ECA makes payment to the exporter under the insurance policy. Finally, the ECA's guarantees are almost always issued directly to a commercial bank, covering the bank's loan to the exporter for preshipment or post-shipment purposes. Alternatively, the guarantee may cover a commercial bank loan to a foreign buyer to help the buyer purchase goods from the ECA's country. In exchange for a guarantee fee paid by the bank, the ECA covers the risks of nonpayment by the exporter or, under the al-ternative form of guarantee, the risk of nonpayment by the foreign buyer if the foreign buyer was the borrower under the bank's loan.

Despite active use of these programs, the ECAs remain a well-kept secret to nonusers, as the ECA managers have been far better at pro-ducing income for exporters and economic benefits for their nations than at publicizing their role and explaining their operations to the general public. The purpose of this book is to uncover the secrets of ECAs and explain the history, programs, functions, and controversies surrounding these pillars of the world's international trading system. Despite their importance, few people even know the names of these organizations or understand their contribution to national growth and development, the problems they have faced and surmounted, and the special nature of their operations that are absolutely essential to the welfare of millions of businesses and hundreds of millions of workers and consumers.

ROLE OF ECAS IN THE WORLD ECONOMY

By any measure, the world's ECAs play a giant role in the national and international economies. On a national level, for example, the world's ECAs finance an average of about 12 percent of their country's exports. In most countries, this is the difference between a national trade surplus and a deficit. Export industries generally are the most dynamic component of a country's economy. They tend to pay higher wages than other industries and support employment growth at a much higher rate than firms pro-ducing solely for the domestic market. Export producers are usually the most efficient in a country because of their need to compete with the world's best companies and are potent transmitters of new technology

Table 1.1
Export Credit Exposure (in billions of U.S. Dollars)

Year	Exposure
1988	290
1989	270
1990	320
1991	370
1992	446
1993	459
1994	504
1995	570
1996	561
1997	508
1998	550

Source: Berne Union and International Monetary Fund (IMF) staff estimates.

and improved management techniques. Exporting companies' tax contributions are significant in every country, and their backward linkages with domestic suppliers of goods and services (which are incorporated in export products) are important contributors to domestic growth.

By the same token, ECAs are essential contributors to the growth and welfare of the international economy. ECAs together financed over $600 billion of world trade in 1996—most of it on relatively short terms of payment. However, at the end of the same year, ECAs also held about $500 billion of medium- and long-term indebtedness from developing and transition countries. This represented more than 24 percent of all foreign indebtedness of these countries.[3]

The ECAs have performed the invaluable function of making credit available to many countries where commercial banks and other private lenders are not willing to make transborder loans, and of making credit available to most developing countries at interest rates and repayment periods that are more favorable than alternative private sources of funds. This has enabled the developing world to purchase much more of the equipment, goods, and services that the industrial countries have to offer, with a resulting dramatic improvement in social welfare, the standard of living, and investment in new infrastructure and the productive sector.

ECAs' transfers of medium- and long-term capital to developing countries rose from about $12 billion in 1976 to $43 billion in 1995. This accounts for 20 to 30 percent of all medium- and long-term debt flows. Table 1.1 depicts the growing value of certain ECAs' short-, medium-, and long-term exposure during the ten years ending in 1998. It covers the activities of only forty-six ECAs, which account for roughly half of total ECA exposure.

The level of export credit agency activity grew rapidly in the early 1990s as international trade increased at a rate approximately three times that of domestic growth. Export trade is now widely acknowledged as the primary engine of economic growth and development and, as such, meritorious of special financial institutions to help with the proper structuring of credit sales, the necessary extension of appropriate loans, the sharing of related risks, and the encouragement of other institutions to participate in this business. In recent years, industrial capacity has expanded, consumer tastes have changed, trade barriers have fallen, and competition among supplier nations has intensified. As a consequence, all countries face growing pressures to adapt their financing systems to new trading requirements.

The current activity levels of individual ECAs vary widely and can be correlated with a number of factors, including the strength and risk appetite of other types of financial institutions, the age and experience of the ECA, the support it receives from public and private sectors, and its geographic region. Export support is highest among Asian ECAs (which financed an average of $15 billion of exports apiece in 1996). In the same year, Western European ECAs supported an average of almost $10 billion of exports per annum, and North American ECAs covered an average of almost $6 billion. African ECAs covered an average of $881 million, Central and Eastern Europe (CEE)/Newly Independent States (NIS) ECAs an average of $276 million, and South American ECAs an average of only $50 million in 1996.

The importance of ECAs in different regions of the world can further be quantified by comparing their support to the total value of gross domestic product (GDP). Asian and Western European ECAs were involved in roughly 2 percent of their countries' GDP in 1996, and Australia/New Zealand ECAs in a little more than 1 percent. North American and CEE/NIS ECAs helped to produce somewhat less than 1 percent of their nations' GDP. By contrast, the ECAs of South America were responsible for less than one-tenth of 1 percent of GDP in 1996, and their relative weakness is believed to be both a cause and an effect of their countries' relatively poor trade performance.

In order to maintain the flow of trade, ECAs are increasingly called upon to finance exports to countries with commercial, economic, and political problems. As a consequence, ECAs' activities continue to grow, while their risks of doing business also rise. Under present and foreseen future circumstances, there is little doubt that the ECAs of the world will be required to play an even greater role than they have in the past. This is because they have proven to be flexible instruments of national policy and effective contributors to international economic development in the face of political uncertainties and rapid changes in trade.

As of 2000, there were nine ECAs in low-income countries, twenty-

Table 1.2
Countries with Officially Supported Export Credit, Guarantee, and Insurance Programs

Developing Countries	Upper Middle Income	Italy
Low Income		Japan
	Argentina	Luxembourg
Bangladesh	Barbados	Netherlands
Ghana	Brazil	New Zealand
India	Chile	Norway
Pakistan	Costa Rica	Portugal
Senegal	Cyprus	Spain
Sri Lanka	Hong Kong	Sweden
Uganda	Iran	Switzerland
Viet Nam	Jordan	United Kingdom
Zambia	Malaysia	United States
	Malta	
Lower Middle Income	Mexico	**Transition Countries**
	Oman	
Bolivia	Sierra Leone	Albania
Cameroon	Singapore	Bosnia-Herzegovina
Colombia	South Africa	Bulgaria
Cote d'Ivoire	South Korea	China
Ecuador	Taiwan	Croatia
El Salvador	Thailand	Czech Republic
Egypt	Trinidad & Tobago	Cuba
Indonesia	Turkey	Estonia
Jamaica	Uruguay	Hungary
Kenya	Venezuela	Kazakstan
Lesotho		Latvia
Liberia	**Industrial Countries**	Lithuania
Mauritius		Moldova
Morocco	Australia	Poland
Nepal	Austria	Romania
Nigeria	Belgium	Russia
Peru	Canada	Slovakia
Philippines	Denmark	Slovenia
Senegal	Finland	Ukraine
Swaziland	France	Uzbekistan
Tunisia	Germany	Yugoslavia
Zimbabwe	Greece	
	Iceland	
	Ireland	
	Israel	

Source: First Washington Associates, Ltd.

two ECAs in lower-middle-income countries, twenty-three ECAs in upper-middle-income countries, twenty-four ECAs in industrial countries, and twenty-one ECAs in transition countries (see Table 1.2). The names of the ECAs in each country are given in Appendix A.

NOTES

1. International Union of Credit and Investment Insurers, *Collection of Histories of Members* (Paris: Berne Union, 1973).

2. National Association of Manufacturers, *Export Financing: A Key to U.S. Export Success* (Washington, DC: NAM, 1994), 1.

3. International Monetary Fund, *Official Financing for Developing Countries* (Washington, DC: IMF, 1998), 11.

Myths and Truths

Many descriptions of export credit agencies (ECAs) are reminiscent of the three blind men describing an elephant. They all knew it was large, but none of them could give an accurate description because they had touched different parts and none had grasped the whole animal. Because of this blindness—or partial vision—regarding ECAs, a number of myths have emerged, which will be explained in this chapter and are summarized in Table 2.1. Some of these myths still apply to a few ECAs, but they are now almost totally invalid if applied to the world's ECAs as a group. Unfortunately, peoples' perceptions of most things tend to lag behind current realities, and it will probably take some time before these widely held myths about ECAs are fully dispelled.

The first myth hypothesizes that ECAs are highly politicized and poorly managed. The reality is that this is true for a small minority of ECAs, as it is for other types of financial institutions, but this is certainly not true of most ECAs. In fact, most ECAs have dedicated, well-educated professional managers and staff who follow sound policies and procedures to maintain a balanced portfolio of risks and appropriate treasury management. The greatest degree of politicization occurred in industrial countries in the 1980s when export credits were approved in the midst of the Third World debt crisis with few prospects for prompt repayment. Since 1990, most of the world's ECAs have substantially improved their managerial practices and have reduced the extent of political influences on their operations.

The second myth is that ECAs subsidize exports by lending at low in-

Table 2.1
Myths about ECAs

1. ECAs are overly politicized and poorly managed
2. ECAs subsidize exports by lending at low interest rates
3. ECAs have high default rates on the credits they support
4. ECAs are unprofitable
5. ECAs distort payment terms by supporting mainly medium-long term credit
6. ECAs substitute for private sources of finance
7. ECAs discourage the development of alternative sources of trade finance
8. ECAs transfer capital out of developing countries
9. ECAs have a negligible effect on exports
10. ECAs have a minor impact on overall economic development

terest rates. This is very old news. Since 1990, all industrial country ECAs have adhered to an Organization for Economic Cooperation and Development (OECD) agreement that they will lend at, or above, market rates of interest. Most developing countries follow this same rule. In the few countries that still lend below market rates, the differential is usually small—1 to 2 percent—and most agree that it will be eliminated altogether in coming years. Only a handful of the world's ECAs still subsidize exports by lending at low interest rates.

A third myth is that ECAs have high defaults on the credits they support. Many industrial country ECAs did have high default rates in the 1980s, but as of 2000, this was largely a thing of the past. Despite the Asian economic crisis of 1997–98, most of the world's ECAs had sustainable default rates. For example, members of the Berne Union, which is an association of 48 ECAs, cumulatively reported claims only slightly in excess of premium income in both 1997 and 1998, and developing country ECAs as a group have always had relatively low defaults on the credits they support. The reasons behind default rates of ECAs in different countries will be explained later.

Another myth is that ECAs are unprofitable. In fact, the overwhelming majority of the world's ECAs are now profitable. The 1999 figures from the Berne Union indicate that industrial country credit insurers were profitable as a group and that only a handful of members remained unprofitable. Almost all developing country ECAs and all privately owned ECAs were profitable in the same year.

Some critics also charge that ECAs distort payment terms by supporting mainly medium to long-term credit. The reality is that the majority of ECA business covered is in the area of short-term credit.[1] The few exceptions are industrial country agencies such as the U.S. Eximbank (Export-Import Bank of the United States). However, it is worth noting that even the U.S. Eximbank did a majority of its business in the short-term area until about 1990. More to the point, almost all developing country ECAs have close to 100 percent of their business in the short-term area—usually under 180 days credit. Under no stretch of the imagination can this be considered to distort payment terms.

The sixth myth is that ECAs substitute for private sources of finance. It is rare for this to happen. A growing number of ECAs are privately owned and those that are not follow a policy of supplementing and complementing and not competing with private sources of finance. This is done by requiring that private banks or the exporters themselves provide the finance that is guaranteed or insured by the ECAs or by providing only second-story rather than direct finance to exporters. If direct finance is provided, many ECAs insist that they will only cover the excess that commercial banks are unwilling to finance.

Myth number seven holds that ECAs discourage the development of alternative sources of trade finance. In fact, ECAs encourage such development. Countries with active ECAs have seen the growth and proliferation of commercial banks as active trade financiers. Export trading companies, export finance companies, and other finance intermediaries also flourish in most countries with ECAs. The availability of ECA services such as guarantees and insurance to spread risks, rediscount programs to ensure liquidity of export loans, credit information to improve knowledge of buyers' creditworthiness, and technical assistance to improve structuring of transactions all help to support private sector providers of trade finance. Also, the demonstration effect of successful ECA operations encourages entrepreneurs in the exporting, banking, and insurance sectors to expand their willingness to finance international business and can ultimately lead them to share or take over functions initially performed wholly by the ECA.

The eighth myth states that ECAs transfer capital out of developing countries. The reality is that the favorable balance of payments effects of an export are only felt when payment is received from abroad. ECAs help to achieve successful exports and payment by proper structuring of credit. Only a small number of developing country ECAs support anything other than short-term credit. This typically has a maximum term of 180 days. It is true that the exporting country does not receive all of the capital transfer until the end of the term offered. However, without the ECA, the country would probably not make the export at all, thus missing 100 percent of the capital benefit rather than just deferring the benefit for a short period. Both exporters and ECAs work to minimize credit terms. There is no evidence that they have anything other than a favorable impact on capital transfers.

Myth number nine holds that ECAs have a negligible effect on exports. However, ECAs now support about $800 billion of exports annually. This is equal to about 12 percent of total exports of the countries in which they are domiciled.[2] Some industrial country ECAs support an even higher percentage of national exports, and most developing country ECAs support a lower percentage. As developing country ECAs gain experience, they generally finance a growing share of exporters' needs.

The tenth myth states that ECAs have a minor impact on overall economic development. The reality is that most governments throughout the world believe the opposite to be true and have proved it by establishing their own ECAs. It is certainly true that ECAs by themselves cannot produce economic development, but in the proper context of other government policies and programs, ECAs are a vital contributor to economic growth and social improvement.

No country has fully succeeded in exporting in the latter half of the twentieth century without establishing an export credit agency. The realities of ECAs have thus overcome the myths, and serious analysts are starting to take note of their massive contribution to economic growth and development.

NOTES

1. International Union of Credit and Investment Insurers, *The Berne Union 1999 Yearbook* (London: Berne Union, 1999), 164.

2. International Montery Fund, *Official Financing for Developing Countries* (Washington, DC, IMF, 1998), 11.

3
Common Features

Export credit agencies (ECAs) around the world share many features, including a common set of objectives, which are both economic and financial.[1] The main economic objectives of ECAs usually include:

- Expand nontraditional exports of private sector goods and services.
- Help to finance nontraditional exporters of all sizes, of all products, and of all regions of the country.
- Provide assistance to indirect exporters to encourage development of linkage industries.
- Supplement and complement, and not compete with, the commercial banks and other private financial institutions.
- Seek to improve the country's balance of payments and to increase domestic employment.
- Help to diversify the products and foreign markets of nontraditional exporters.
- Improve the financial skills of nontraditional exporters and reduce their risks in extending credit to foreign buyers.
- Increase the knowledge and sophistication of the country's banks in the area of export credit.
- Encourage the national insurance industry to participate in coverage of the risks of nonpayment of export credits.
- Provide assistance for exports that are deemed to be in the national interest.

- Help national firms to make investments abroad in order to increase the nation's foreign exchange earnings.
- Seek to match officially supported foreign financial competition.

The main financial objectives of ECAs usually include:

- Realize a profit for shareholders.
- Support only operations that offer a reasonable assurance of repayment.
- Operate in a businesslike fashion.
- Mobilize funds from domestic and foreign sources to finance national exports.
- Ensure that programs offering a lesser return on capital are offset by programs offering a greater return.
- Charge interest rates and other fees that are sufficient to cover related costs.
- Strive to increase the real value of the organization's capital over time, to serve as a basis for expanded operations.
- Manage investments to maximize returns, consistent with security of payment and cash flow requirements.
- Ensure the availability of funds to make prompt disbursements as required on loans, guarantees, and insurance.
- Conclude coinsurance and reinsurance agreements to limit the possibility of catastrophic losses.
- Follow sound principles of risk-sharing and maintaining a balanced portfolio.
- Maintain a conservative relationship of capital and reserves to actual and contingent liabilities.

Just as they share objectives, ECAs around the world share a number of constraints, imposed by such factors as their total authority and yearly budgetary ceilings, by requirements that they supplement and complement and not compete with private finance, by the need to seek reasonable likelihood of repayment on transactions, by other limits imposed to ensure prudent financial management, by the need to conform to the terms and conditions of international understandings, and by a number of other restrictions imposed by their authorizing legislation, guardian authorities in government, or private shareholders. The ECAs' own financial condition—particularly the size of their capital and reserves—serves to limit the total amount of exports they can support. A final major constraint is the size of the ECAs' trained staff. Executives, managers, officers, and technicians who are skilled in export credit matters are in very short supply, and their availability represents a severe constraint upon the expansion of ECA operations in most countries.

Official export credit, guarantee, and insurance agencies also share many features with regard to the mechanics of their operations. They

Table 3.1
Typical Repayment Terms, by Contract Price

Contract Value	Maximum Term
Up to $80,000	2 years
$80,001 to $175,000	3 years
$175,001 to $350,000	4 years
Over $350,000	5 years

Source: Export-Import Bank of the United States.

have similar eligibility criteria, term differentiation, risk classification, degree of coverage, underwriting techniques, premium and interest rate systems, policy administration, risk-sharing methods, and reinsurance. This is not an accident. The techniques, terms, and conditions of export credit insurance and guarantees have been largely "internationalized" by regular exchanges of information and agreements reached through the International Union of Credit and Investment Insurers (Berne Union) and the Organization for Economic Cooperation and Development (OECD), and there is a growing level of comparability among individual national schemes.

ECAs can help finance short-, medium-, or long-term transactions, and the conditions of financing assistance are usually quite different depending on the tenor. A short-term transaction is usually defined as up to one year, medium-term as one to five years and long-term as over five years. The OECD Agreement on Export Credit currently limits the maximum term to ten years.

Repayment terms supported by ECAs around the world tend to be similar, since they are based upon competitive realities and the needs of importing customers. Most financing is short term, with a maximum period of one year. However, larger sales of manufactured goods, particularly capital equipment and consumer durables, may receive longer terms dependent on contract price (see Table 3.1).

Major projects and multimillion-dollar equipment sales are often financed on terms of five to ten years. Also, certain products routinely receive terms longer than five years. For example, twin-engine turbo-powered aircraft, including executive jets, are typically financed on a seven-year term. Ships receive an eight-year term, and commercial jet aircraft may be financed by ECAs on a ten to twelve-year term.

Normally, export credit agencies provide assistance that does not exceed 90 percent of postshipment financing, with the exporter or bank taking the balance of the risk for its own account. Pre-shipment assistance is also usually limited to a maximum of 90 percent of required credit. On medium- and long-term transactions, official schemes require the foreign buyer to make an advance payment of at least 15 percent. On short-term coverage, no advance payment is required from the foreign buyer.

A number of different premium systems are employed by credit insurance schemes. On medium- and long-term transactions, the premiums are normally a function of country, term, and type of buyer (public or private). On short-term transactions, premiums may be based on such things as experience with the exporter, volume, size of the deductible, country spread, and average term. Some or all of these factors are taken into consideration by every official scheme, with greater or lesser weight being given to individual components.

Interest rates on ECAs' loans are much less subject to variance for individual transactions. They are usually the same for all credits and are normally at fixed rates of interest, related to prevailing market rates of interest.

Governments play many roles in support of ECAs. They can be insurers or reinsurers of risks; they can provide finance to exporters or to their customers; or they can intervene in the cost of financing. It is important to note that government's role in most ECAs is now diminishing, as the private sector in most countries is more willing and able to take risks and assist ECAs in their activities. Growing private extensions of export credit have reduced the need for official export finance in many countries, and decreases in the volume of mixed credits (a combination of trade and aid financing) have further limited the necessity for government loans to support exports. However, governments are still actively involved in risk-sharing with ECAs in all countries. Even though international private reinsurance of export credit risks continue to grow, governments are still the major insurers or reinsurers of risk, particularly political risks, for their national ECAs.

KEY FACTORS FOR SUCCESS OF EXPORT CREDIT AGENCIES

Based on experience with ECAs around the world, twelve elements have been identified as common features in their success:[2]

Capital Adequacy

The most successful ECAs have substantial paid-in capital, which is invested in interest-bearing securities. Investment earnings are sufficient to keep the ECA profitable even during the first few years of operation, when operating revenues are relatively low. Capital is equal to at least 25 percent of anticipated outstanding loans, guarantees, and insurance for the early years of operation and gradually declines as a percentage of outstandings in subsequent years.

Organizational Autonomy

Organizational autonomy is very important. Successful ECAs have the authority to make their own decisions, guided solely by their managers and board of directors. They do not make business decisions for political reasons only and are not required by government to undertake unprofitable operations unless the ECA is acting as agent for the government using government funds or committing the government to the related risk.

Support from Government

Support, or at least benign neglect, from government is a hallmark of successful ECAs. This support is primarily in the form of assuming political risk coverage but may also consist of the provision of funds on favorable terms, the availability of government guarantees to cover lending operations, publicity given the ECA by government agencies, as well as other forms of encouragement given by the government to use the ECA programs.

Proper Risk-Sharing

Vital to success is an ECA's requirement that commercial banks and exporters share risks in every transaction. Also, the best ECAs limit losses by coinsurance and reinsurance agreements with their own governments, with foreign reinsurance companies, and with other ECAs. Political risk assumption by government can be an essential condition for success.

Appropriate Fee Structure

Successful ECAs operate on the principle that availability of funds is more important to the exporter than cost and that an ECA must be profitable over the long run in order to survive. Accordingly, interest rates and premiums reflect the real costs of doing business and maintaining the value of capital. Interest rates are market-based, and guarantee and insurance premiums are designed to cover related claims and administrative expenses.

Diversity of Operations

In order to be fully successful, the best ECAs offer a full range of products, including loans, guarantees, insurance, and technical assistance. The need for, and use of, these programs will vary over time, as will their profitability. By offering all types of programs, the ECA maximizes its impact on exports and cushions low returns in some areas with higher returns in others. Also, the programs are mutually supporting. For example, technical assistance can reduce risks and improve repayment of transactions that are supported by loans, guarantees, or insurance.

Quality of Management

The most successful ECAs are run by finance professionals who have extensive prior experience with the management of private financial institutions. They are thoroughly familiar with the techniques of trade finance and are flexible, efficient, profit-conscious managers. In order to obtain and keep such individuals, the ECA provides compensation comparable to that in private sector banks.

Efficiency of Procedures

Paperwork and administrative procedures are simple and straightforward in the best ECAs. Average processing time for loans, guarantees, and insurance is five days or less, and internal analysis is often confined to a checklist procedure rather than memowriting. Discretionary commitment authority is given to officers within the organization, and delegated authority is given to exporters and banks, depending upon the risks they are willing to take and the procedures they follow.

Aggressive Marketing

Marketing is a constant feature of ECAs, and is designed to familiarize banks and exporters with ECA programs and encourage their use. Marketing is directed to all types and sizes of exporters and to all geographic regions of the country and is frequently done through third parties, such as banks and trade associations.

Skill in Credit Analysis

Successful ECAs have loan officers and underwriters with sound judgment, extensive experience, and mastery of the techniques of risk analysis. Losses due to inadequate analysis in the early years are gradually reduced as the ECA learns from its mistakes and upgrades its skills.

Appropriate Collateral and Guarantees

Collateral and guarantee requirements of successful ECAs follow generally accepted business practices in the markets they enter. Security requirements take into account competitive realities and the practicality of enforcing collateral rights. Underwriting policy emphasizes taking security consistent with acceptable risk parameters for the whole portfolio.

Technical Sophistication

The best ECAs utilize the latest financing techniques and instruments, changing those techniques and instruments as necessary to match foreign competition. These ECAs make every effort to transfer their knowledge of financial innovations and successful risk management to their nations' banks and exporters.

NOTES

1. Export-Import Bank of India, *Export Credit Agencies Around the World: A Comparative Analysis* (Bombay, India: Eximbank of India, 1994).

2. First Washington Associates, *Recommendations for a Model Export Finance System* (Arlington, VA: FWA, 1992), 32–36.

4

Programs

The availability of credit at a reasonable price and on appropriate payment terms is a key element in the success of exporting firms. Credit is necessary at the preshipment stage to enable the exporter to meet working capital needs and to purchase, manufacture, and pack the goods destined for export. Preshipment financing also helps to meet administrative expenses and overhead requirements during the period prior to export. Such preshipment financing gains extra importance when a firm must stockpile substantial inventories of raw materials, semifinished or finished goods due to problems in receiving imported requirements, or in shipping goods overseas (because of shipping schedules, foreign exchange problems, distance from the source of supply or purchaser, etc.).

At the postshipment stage, credit is required to bridge the gap between shipment of the goods and the receipt of payment from the overseas buyer. Usually, such payment is received in a matter of days or weeks, but increasingly, sellers of all types of goods are being asked by their overseas customers to provide more extended credit to permit the buyers to realize some economic gain from their purchases before they have to make payment to the exporters.

Investment credit is often not available at all for new and small producers, or only available at such short terms of repayment as to make an investment in fixed assets appear uneconomic. A major finding of First Washington Associates (FWA) studies has been that the availability of credit is much more important than its cost. The availability of bank

Figure 4.1
The Export Cycle

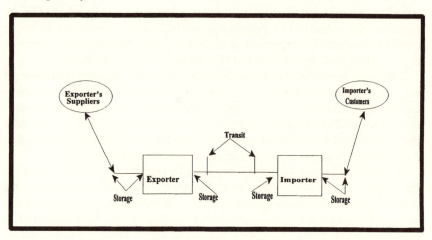

credit for exporters in turn permits them to make advances to local sub-suppliers, or indirect exporters, to help meet the latter's financing requirements. In many developing countries, such advance or progress payments constitute the main source of external financing for indirect exporters.

The programs of export credit agencies (ECAs) are constructed to meet the special needs of exporters. These needs typically extend throughout the production-shipment-payment cycle that an exporter experiences and for which credit is required (see Figure 4.1). It is normal for an exporter to have to pay cash immediately to its suppliers at the start of the cycle and then have to wait until the importer's customers have paid the importer and the importer then pays the exporter. This cycle usually takes less than 180 days, but if export goods take a long time to manufacture, stay in storage a long time, or take a long time for the importer to sell and receive sales proceeds, the cycle can be considerably longer. Some exporters have enough retained earnings so that they can self-finance such transactions, but most exporters find it necessary to seek external financing to carry their business.

The bulk of international trade, particularly for commodities and consumer goods, is still financed largely on a cash, open account, or letter of credit basis between buyer and seller, without the support of ECAs. In these cases, commercial banks or the exporters provide the necessary credit to foreign buyers.[1] Exporters of manufactured goods, however, often require substantial assistance from ECAs, consisting of credit insurance as well as official refinancing facilities. The incidence and intensity of such support has expanded in line with the increasing complexity and cost of these exports, particularly capital goods, whose sales often require larger credits and longer terms than the private sector is prepared to extend without official support. Furthermore, a number of ECAs facilitate the extension of pre-shipment financing to exporters to lower costs of production, improve international competitiveness, and encourage the development of nontraditional forms of export activity.

Both commercial and political risks are present in dealing with foreign buyers, and the incidence of countrywide delays, defaults, and reschedulings of foreign debt add an extra dimension of risk to export transactions. One of the most important functions of ECAs is helping to cover these risks and showing the private sector how to implement intelligent risk management procedures in their overseas credit sales.

The kind of export financing required or received is closely related to the type of goods or services being exported, the use to which they are put, the nature of the overseas buyer, the country of destination, and the size of the exporting firm. The type of product being exported is very closely related to the length of financing term. Raw materials, parts, semi-finished products, and consumer goods traditionally receive a repayment term of up to 180 days, agricultural products up to one year, motor vehicles up to three years, and capital equipment up to five years. Large sales of capital equipment embodied in major projects may receive a repayment term in excess of five years, up to a maximum of ten years.

The nature of the overseas buyer is also important in determining credit terms. For example, if sales are made to overseas dealers and distributors, they typically receive a somewhat shorter term than if they are made directly to end users. More importantly, if the overseas buyer is a subsidiary of the exporter, credit terms may be either shorter or longer than sales to nonrelated companies, depending on overall corporate strategy at the time.

Longer terms may be justified in certain types of sales by the special cash-flow characteristics of the project in question or by the need to match officially supported foreign competition. In general, developing countries request and receive longer terms of export credit than industrial countries. This appears to be largely because official ECAs recognize the need to help the balance of payments of less-developed country borrowers, a principle recognized in the OECD (Organization for Economic Cooperation and Development) Consensus on Export Credit, which establishes maximum terms and minimum interest rates based on country of destination.

Finally, the size of the exporting firm seems to be related to the term of export finance inasmuch as smaller firms are usually direct exporters of things such as raw materials, parts, semifinished products, and consumer goods, which have shorter terms of payment. Larger exporting firms may obtain longer terms because they are exporters of major amounts of capital goods or of projects requiring an extended period in which to repay associated financing.

There are a number of factors that make selling abroad on credit terms riskier than selling domestically. Reliable information on foreign buyers from third parties is usually harder to obtain, and it is therefore more difficult to assess creditworthiness. General industry or sector trends may also be less well known, and an exporter does not benefit from the inside knowledge about his or her buyer that comes from the close daily contact on an informal basis that is available between domestic firms. In the event of default on credit, exporters are further disadvantaged by their distance from the buyer and the lack of a local presence. It is usually more complicated and costly to enforce payment or bring suit, and exporters may not be equitably treated in the courts of the buyer's country.

In addition to commercial risks such as delayed payment, default, insolvency, and bankruptcy, export credit sales involve significant political risks that are beyond the control of both buyer and seller. Such political risks involve war, riot, revolution, expropriation, shortage of foreign exchange, and other transfer problems, which may impede payment after shipment of the goods to the buyer's country. Another category of political risk is the failure of a public buyer to repay its export credit, for whatever reason. All such buyers are owned by governments and thus all risks of nonpayment are classified as political. The commercial and political risks enumerated are typically covered by export credit insurance. The cancellation of export or import licenses is also often part of standard political risk coverage.

Virtually all export credit insurance and guarantee schemes charge premiums that are designed to cover all administrative expenses, establish reserves sufficient to meet anticipated claims, and at least break even or make a small profit on an operational basis (not including the interest earned on reserves). Most schemes lose money in the first few years of operation because of a relatively low premium base and the costs of design and start up, often combined with a failure to attract more creditworthy customers. It is essential to offer good service in the form of speedy underwriting decisions and rapid and fair claims processing. Policies must be straightforward and as comprehensive as possible, and personnel must be well informed and helpful.

Even if these preconditions are met, it has often been difficult for ECAs to build up a large and well-balanced business that can be profitable. Even those agencies that have achieved long-term profitability have had to be prepared for short-run periods of problem loans, heavy claims, and associated unprofitability, which are usually caused by economic problems in buying countries, which preclude prompt repayment of export credits. ECAs have tried to insulate themselves against such problems by getting as diversified a risk portfolio as possible (in terms of exporters, types of goods, buyers, and countries covered), guarding as much as possible against "adverse selection" against them of risks which their customers want them to cover, trying to achieve "whole turnover" of exporters' sales where possible, making sound individual underwriting decisions, spreading the risk on covered transactions between themselves and the exporters and banks, obtaining reinsurance if possible from other agencies, and adjusting premiums to maintain proper reserves and profitability.

The main types of loan, guarantee and insurance programs offered by ECAs are as follows:[2]

1. *Pre-Shipment Insurance*. Pre-shipment insurance is issued directly to exporters and is totally different from pre-shipment guarantees, which are issued to banks and will be discussed subsequently. Pre-shipment insurance covers mainly political risks to which exporters are exposed during the period between conclusion of a sales contract or acceptance of an order and shipment of the related goods.

The coverage is usually for a lower percentage than for post-shipment risks and typically is limited to the contract price (less discounts) less all expenses saved by nonfulfillment of the contract, and amounts received toward payment and amounts that the buyer would have been entitled to take into account by way of credit, set-off, or counter claim.

Pre-shipment coverage typically excludes contract repudiation, including unwillingness to accept the products or goods by the buyer. It is usually limited to coverage for insolvency of the buyer, war risks, government intervention, and export or import embargo.

Pre-shipment insurance is not a heavily used product in most countries and is of only limited usefulness to most exporters, due to unfamiliarity with the product, very restricted terms of coverage, relatively high cost, normally short period of validity, and exporters' feeling of relative comfort with the risks to which they are exposed during the period prior to shipment, together with their physical possession of the goods that are being insured during this period.

The types of goods that are most often covered by pre-shipment export credit insurance are those requiring an extended period of manufacture, with high value added, for large contract amounts and for sales to countries where political risks are perceived to be high and/or the exporter has little or no experience.

The period of coverage for pre-shipment insurance is typically less than 180 days, but in the case of heavy machinery and equipment forming part of a major project, which is specially manufactured for a particular customer, pre-shipment coverage may extend to one year or, occasionally, longer.

Many export credit insurers in recent years have found that the major demand for pre-shipment coverage is to cover sales to Eastern Europe and Central Asia. Such coverage is rarely issued in isolation from some kind of support for the post-shipment financing, which typically involves large amounts of money and long repayment terms.

2. *Short-Term Post-Shipment Insurance.* This is the most widely used and popular form of export credit insurance. For most ECAs around the world, short-term post-shipment coverage accounts for a majority of their business.

This insurance is typically offered in a global or whole turnover policy, valid for one year, covering all of an exporter's credit sales to eligible markets. Many ECAs, particularly privately owned ones, require a first-loss deductible as a feature of the policy, and it is common to grant the exporter a discretionary credit limit, or DCL, giving the exporter coverage for any buyer up to the amount of the limit without the necessity to obtain the insurer's specific approval of the buyer's creditworthiness. The exporter is usually required to pay a minimum premium for the global policy and is required to file monthly reports on insured shipments, together with the appropriate premium payment.

Most export credit insurers cover 80 to 90 percent of short-term credit sales, but as special export promotion incentives, a few of the industrial country, publicly owned credit insurers have recently offered coverage of 95 percent and even 100 percent. This policy is now being reconsidered by ECA managers as it violates two fundamental principles of insurance: that the insured party share in the risks, so that it will be more cautious in credit extension and more involved in credit recovery, and that the insurer seek to spread the risks so that it is not the only party exposed.

Many insurers quote a single, composite premium rate for short-term post-shipment coverage. Other insurers' short-term rates vary, depending on the type of instrument being covered (i.e., letter of credit, open account, etc.) and/or maturity (i.e., 90 days, 180 days, etc.). It is usual for the insurer to grant a discount off standard rates for exporters with a history of good repayment experience.

Some export credit insurers will cover short-term sales on a transaction-by-transaction basis, charging higher premiums to account for the lack of a spread of risk and the probability that these transactions are riskier than the norm. Many insurers also offer consignment risk coverage for goods sold to dealers and distributors in foreign countries, where title is held by the exporter until the goods are resold to an end user or consumer. Consignment risk coverage is limited to political risks.

All types of goods are covered by short-term post-shipment insurance, including heavy machine tools and capital equipment. However, in most countries a majority of short-term post-shipment cover goes for primary materials, parts, components, semifinished goods and consumer goods. Most exporters seek short-term credit insurance primarily to cover the political risks of selling to developing countries. However, the coverage of commercial risks can also be extremely significant, and many exporters' banks have insisted that the firms obtain this type of insurance and assign the proceeds to the banks as a way of protecting the related financing.

3. *Medium- to Long-Term Post-Shipment Insurance.* Medium-term coverage and long-term coverage are usually handled very similarly by export credit insurers. However, it is noteworthy that private export credit insurers have much tighter limitations on the maximum term that they can cover, so that almost all long-term coverage is handled by the official insurers. For either medium or long-term coverage, the insurers typically require a minimum cash payment from the buyer of 15 percent, so that the financed portion does not exceed 85 percent. Of the latter amount, the insurers will normally cover 80 to 90 percent.

The finance contracts relating to medium- and long-term sales specify a rate of interest to be paid, either on a fixed or floating basis. Most export credit insurers will cover some or all of this interest in addition to principal. Almost all medium- and long-term coverage is issued on a transaction basis, after careful inspection of the buyer's creditworthiness. For longer-term transactions, it is usual for the insurer to inspect not only the buyer's current and previous financial condition and record of payment, but also to require projections of operational and financial performance.

Many export credit insurers relate maximum terms of payment for medium-term transactions to the contract price of goods shipped, with longer terms for larger transactions. For long-term deals, the maximum terms of payment are set for the OECD countries by the Consensus on Export Credits. In contrast to short-term export credits, most banks feel a need for insurance or similar coverage for all medium- and long-term credits to developing or emerging countries. This is because extended time horizons for payment invariably stimulate perceptions of greater risk.

Premiums for medium-term coverage are based upon the initial amount of principal outstanding and are usually a function of the repayment term, foreign market, and/or type of buyer (public, private). Medium-term premiums are typically paid in one sum, up front, at the beginning of the transaction. By contrast, long-term premiums are mainly paid on a retroactive basis, at the same time that payments of principal and interest are due on the insured credit based upon the declining balance of principal outstanding.

4. *Overseas Investment Insurance.* Related to export credit insurance, is overseas investment insurance. This type of coverage is typically offered by export credit insurers and covers investors' direct equity investments in foreign ventures. The risks typically covered by investment insurance

are war and related political disturbances, government expropriation, and currency inconvertibility. The insurance normally covers the initial equity investment, whether in the form of cash, exported goods, or services, plus some amount of annual earnings on the initial investment. Policies may be available for just one or two, or for all, of the risk categories previously mentioned. Many insurers disaggregate premiums, depending on which risks are covered. Some insurers do not permit a choice of risk groups to be covered and charge a composite premium for the combined coverage.

5. *Overseas Lease Insurance*. Overseas lease insurance is a product that is not heavily used because it is tailored mainly to equipment exporters in industrial countries that have tax laws favoring this type of transaction. The insurance offered may cover either (1) operating leases in which payments total less than the full value of the leased product, a residual value remains at the end of the lease, and the lessor intends to repossess the product; or (2) financing leases in which payments equal or exceed the value of the product, little residual value remains at lease-end, and ownership is transferred to the lessee.

For operating leases, insurance is typically in two parts, which may be purchased jointly or separately. The first part covers political and commercial risks that may affect the stream of payments due on the leased product. The second part is coverage against government prevention of repossession. For financing leases, coverage is usually for both political and commercial risks affecting the stream of payments. There is no separate coverage for residual value. Generally, lease terms of up to five years may be covered, although longer terms are sometimes permitted. Most insurers do not require a cash payment for an operating lease but do require a minimum cash payment of 15 percent for a financing lease. The percentage insured in both cases is normally 80 to 90 percent, with the exporter covering the balance of the risk on its own account.

Lease insurance is written on a transaction-by-transaction basis and the premium rate charged is typically governed by the country, length of transaction, and type of lessee (public, private). Lease insurance has been most heavily utilized for products like transport equipment (airplanes, trucks, buses, etc.) and construction equipment. It usually involves industrial country lessors and industrial or upper-tier developing country lessees.

6. *Performance Bond Coverage*. Many export credit insurers issue policies covering the exporter against losses resulting from a foreign buyer's wrongful calling of a standby letter of credit or bank guarantee issued as a bid, performance, or advance payment guarantee. This type of insurance usually covers contracts involving a government buyer. Insurers generally require that the underlying contract contain a clearly specified dispute resolution procedure and that the exporter invoke that procedure

to establish that a calling was wrongful. Coverage under these policies is typically 80 to 90 percent of the award or amount of costs in dispute. Claims may be payable if the dispute resolution procedure yields an award in favor of the insured, and the insured is unable to collect the award; if the resolution procedure cannot proceed because the foreign buyer has refused to participate; or if an award in favor of the buyer can be proven to have been obtained through corruption or duress.

The term of performance bond coverage is generally equal to the term of the underlying letter of credit or guarantee, plus an additional period to accommodate the possibility of extensions or delays. Most of these insurance policies are for periods of less than one year, but for large projects, it is not uncommon for them to extend up to three years or occasionally longer. Premium rates are generally considerably lower than standard forms of export credit insurance, and it is often the case that bid guarantee coverage is slightly less expensive than performance, advance payment, and other guarantees, reflecting lower claims experience with the former.

Performance bond insurance has been most heavily used by the construction industry. Insurance for these bonds was initially concentrated on exports of construction services to the Middle Eastern countries, but bond requirements for internationally bid projects have now spread to all areas of the world, and many exporters besides engineers and contractors are required to post these types of performance assurances with overseas buyers.

7. *Pre-shipment Guarantees.* Pre-shipment guarantees are issued to commercial banks to encourage them to lend to exporters. These guarantees cover loans extended to meet working capital needs during the production of goods for export. In the developing countries, firms of all sizes may benefit from pre-shipment guarantees, but it is more normal for the beneficiaries to be small and medium enterprises, exporters of new products, and exporters to new markets. In the industrial countries, many pre-shipment guarantee programs are restricted to small businesses only.

It is important to remember that pre-shipment guarantees protect only the lender from default by the exporter. They do not cover the exporter should the foreign buyer default in its payment; this latter risk is normally covered by export credit insurance. Pre-shipment guarantees normally cover loans with a maximum term of 180–365 days. These loans may cover working capital needs for a single export or revolving loans covering all working capital needs for multiple exports during a one-year period.

The proceeds of loans covered by pre-shipment guarantees may be used to purchase finished products or materials, products, services, and labor to produce goods for current or future export sales. Alternatively, many agencies encourage the proceeds of such loans to be used to market products, participate in trade fairs, or conduct other promotional activities aimed at developing export sales. Typically, the pre-shipment guarantee covers 85 to 90 percent of the principal amount of the loan, plus some agreed portion of the interest thereon. It is normal to require related inventories and accounts receivable as collateral and fairly standard to require the personal guarantees of the exporter's owners additionally. It is also standard practice to require an export order or letter of credit as a precondition for issuance of the guarantee.

Pre-shipment guarantee fees are typically lower than post-shipment fees, but this is not always the case since the exporters being guaranteed are usually not viewed by the banks as highly creditworthy—they are usually small and may lack a sufficient record of performance. Some pre-shipment guarantee programs provide more advantageous coverage for smaller, newer exporters but insist that after a certain point they are no longer eligible for this treatment and must "graduate" to a more commercially structured program. The obvious advantage of pre-shipment guarantees is that they serve to introduce newer and smaller exporters to the benefits of commercial bank financing by adding the creditworthiness of the guarantee agency to that of the exporter. The disadvantage is that the guarantee adds extra paperwork and processing time to that required by the bank.

8. *Post-Shipment Guarantees.* Post-shipment guarantees can cover short-, medium-, or long-term loans but typically are confined to the last two categories. These guarantees are issued directly to financing banks and usually cover loans in which the obligor is the foreign buyer but which are disbursed to the account of the exporter. Medium- or long-term guarantees usually require that the buyer make a cash payment of at least 15 percent and that the financing bank share in some portion of the risk on its loan. However, as noted previously, 100 percent coverage is sometimes offered by the guarantor, particularly if public buyers are involved or if the transaction is long term. Some major guarantee programs offer authority to participating banks to commit the guarantee without first checking with the guarantor, under predetermined terms and conditions, provided the bank will take a higher portion of the risk for its own account.

Post-shipment guarantees usually cover individual, specifically identified export transactions involving one exporter and one buyer. However, medium-term post-shipment guarantees are also used to cover repetitive sales by an exporter to its overseas dealer or distributor, and long-term post-shipment guarantees often cover major projects in which there is one buyer but many exporters. Also, medium-term guarantees are used to cover lines of credit to foreign banks in which numerous individual exporters sell to numerous foreign buyers.

9. *Inflation Risk Insurance.* Inflation risk insurance was extensively used

by the French and to a lesser extent by other ECAs in the 1970s and 1980s. Coverage was offered against increases in costs during the manufacturing period of export contracts and was generally limited to contracts of a minimum size, with developing country borrowers, in which the manufacturing period exceeded twelve months.

Price variations were calculated in accordance with official price indices, and exporters were usually compensated for all cost increases beyond a first-loss margin. In the 1970s and 1980s, the first-loss margin was often deliberately set low, or was nonexistent, as a conscious means of subsidizing the exporter. Premiums for this type of coverage were also generally very low, usually around 1 percent per annum. In recent years, the value of this type of coverage has declined significantly as most countries, both developing and industrial, have maintained better control over domestic cost inflation, and the technique of inflation risk insurance is rarely utilized nowadays.

10. *Exchange Risk Insurance*. Exchange risk insurance provides an exporter with coverage when the export contract is denominated in a foreign currency and that currency depreciates in value against the exporter's own currency prior to the receipt of payment for goods sold. The period of coverage is typically up to one year, but may be as long as five years in some cases.

The premium depends on the length of cover and the foreign currency. If the exporter's currency appreciates against the foreign currency and the exporter thus receives less local currency than originally anticipated, a claim is payable by the insurer. On the other hand, if the exporter's currency depreciates against the foreign currency of contract, many insurers require the exporter to pay them the resulting profit. Because of the suddenness and magnitude of exchange rate movements, exchange risk insurance can produce great fluctuations in an ECA's claims payments. As this is not affected by creditworthiness of the borrower or normal political risks covered by credit insurance, exchange risk insurance is offered by very few ECAs.

Exchange risk insurance is of greatest value to industrial country exporters whose own currencies are appreciating against foreign currencies in which contracts have traditionally been denominated. In practical fact, it has been most utilized by European exporters who have denominated their contracts in dollars to meet customer preference.

11. *Trade Fair Insurance*. A few ECAs provide a subsidized insurance policy to encourage exporters to participate in overseas trade fairs, shows, and missions. A trade fair insurance policy typically covers the cost of sending goods and personnel to the trade fair and in some cases may cover costs of advertising, promotion, and other overseas marketing.

Such policies are typically issued or assigned to commercial banks and permit a generous repayment term sufficient to amortize all related costs. In some cases, the exporter is not required to repay the entire loan, and the ECA makes up the difference with a pre-planned claim payment. Most such thinly disguised subsidies have been phased out by ECAs, but it is still common for export credit insurers to charge very low premiums for this special inducement to export.

12. *Local-Cost and Third-Country Cost Insurance*. Many credit insurers offer assistance with the coverage of local costs and third-country costs related to exports from their countries. Third country costs, representing parts or components in an export product or project that come from a country other than the exporter's or buyer's country, are typically insured on the same basis as other parts of the export. However, limits are usually set on the maximum percentage of contract price, which can comprise third-country costs, and if they exceed this limit, the transaction may be structured so that third-country costs are handled separately from the ECA-supported portion.

Local costs of an export project are rarely supported by developing country ECAs but are often insured by industrial country ECAs, particularly when a major project is involved and advantageous long-term financing is an important competitive element. Industrial country insurers typically will cover local-cost financing as an important competitive element. In such cases, coverage is offered for local cost financing equal to the cash payment for the export, usually 15 percent.

The repayment term for local-cost financing is usually shorter than that for the export itself, with a maximum of five years being the norm. By contrast, the repayment term for third-country costs is almost always identical to, and undifferentiated from, the term for national content of export costs. The premiums payable for both local costs and third-country costs are normally figured on the same basis as national content of export costs.

The percentage of third-country costs that each insurer will cover varies considerably. Private insurers rarely impose any requirement in this area. Many public insurers in developing countries similarly fail to specify limits. In the industrial countries, many official insurers specify that national content must be at least 50 percent for short-term sales and 70 to 85 percent for medium- to long-term sales.

13. *Buyer Credits*. Buyer credits are authorized by ECAs in favor of the foreign buyer of exported goods and services, which has full responsibility for repayment of the credit. The buyer credit is typically documented by a loan agreement, promissory note, and other legal papers. It is disbursed at the direction of the buyer to one or more exporters— typically the former if just one large product is involved, or the latter if a major project is being financed.

Buyer credits usually cover a maximum of 85 percent of contract price, with the requirement for a cash payment of at least 15 percent. They may be issued in isolation from, or in conjunction with, commercial bank financing for a portion of the contract price. Increasingly, buyer credits are offered as part of a package of financing arranged by a multilateral development bank, which involves procurement from a number of countries.

Repayment terms for buyer credits are typically medium to long term, with the latter accounting for a majority of the value of these credits. If a commercial bank is involved as cofinancier, it is not unusual for the bank loan to be repaid on a shorter term than the ECA credit. Repayment is usually scheduled in equal semiannual installments of principal beginning after a grace period that extends six months after product delivery, project completion, or start-up. Interest is usually charged at a fixed rate throughout the repayment term and is payable semiannually beginning six months after disbursement, based on the declining principal balance outstanding from time to time.

Exceptionally, interest may be capitalized during construction and added to the principal balance, which is repaid starting after expiration of the grace period. Or, the direct loan contract may authorize equal payments of principal and interest after the grace period, which in effect lowers cash requirements during the early years of debt repayment.

14. *Lines of Credit*. Lines of credit are devices used by ECAs to "bundle" multiple export credit transactions of different exporters using one obligor of record. The objective is to lower administrative costs, simplify and standardize paperwork, and ensure that the obligor is creditworthy. Also, by aggregating many export sales into one line of credit, a rationale can be advanced for permitting more generous terms of payment.

Lines of credit are usually authorized by the ECA in favor of a financial institution in the buying country. The line is evidenced by a credit agreement between the ECA and the foreign financial institution. The latter takes responsibility for deciding what individual buyers and export transactions to finance under the line and agrees with the ECA on the terms of credit that will be extended to the buyers. The foreign financial institution takes full responsibility for repaying all disbursements made under the line, regardless of whether or not its credit extensions are repaid by the foreign buyers in question. Disbursements under the line are made directly to exporters in the ECA's country in accordance with instructions from the foreign financial institution.

Lines of credit typically call for repayment in the medium- to long-term range, sometimes with a grace period of one to two years. They are frequently used by ECAs wishing to help their exporters enter new markets or for sales to markets that are perceived to pose extra payment problems for small transactions.

15. *Tied Aid Credits*. Tied aid credits are those in which the donor coun-

try subsidizes the cost of credit to the foreign buyer as an inducement to purchase its goods and services, either by extending the repayment period or lowering the interest rate of a standard export credit or by combining a standard export credit with a concessional loan or grant ("mixed credit").

Tied aid is typically authorized and administered by a country's official export credit agency or, in the case of mixed credits, they are coordinated by the ECA. When a mixed credit is involved, separate agreements are signed for the standard export credit and the concessional loan or grant. The credits are disbursed directly to suppliers upon shipment of goods or in progress payments if an extended fabrication or construction period is required.

Mixed or otherwise, tied aid credits are typically used for major projects perceived to be in the national interest, in developing countries where competition between supplier nations is intense, or in foreign markets that used to be colonies of the ECA's country, and special efforts are made to improve the terms of financing. Almost always, tied aid credits involve sales to public buyers in developing countries. The regions receiving most tied aid, in order are Asia, Africa, the Middle East, and Latin America. The countries receiving the most tied aid have been China, India, and Indonesia. The types of projects most often financed by tied aid are power, transport, telecommunications, other capital goods, and extractive industries.

NOTES

1. Harry M. Venedikian, and Gerald A. Warfield, *Global Trade Financing* (New York: John Wiley & Sons, 2000), chap. 2.

2. Organization for Economic Cooperation and Development, *Export Credit Financing Systems in OECD Member and Non-Member Countries* (Paris: OECD Publications, 1993 [Rev. 1999]).

5

Rationales

Six types of economic justification, or rationales have been advanced in support of export credit agencies. The first is that they are a means of responding to imperfections in the capital and money markets, which distort all assistance to exporters. Second, ECA programs are viewed as a response to capital market deficiencies, which are biased against the extension of medium- to long-term assistance as opposed to short-term credit. Third, ECAs are justified by their direct contribution to wages, production, and employment and their indirect contribution to linkage industries, tax revenues, and so on. Fourth, ECAs are justified for their special assistance to new and small firms, new products, and new export markets, which would otherwise be neglected by private finance. A fifth rationale for some ECAs is that they serve in lieu of aid programs for developing countries. The sixth justification for each national ECA is that it is required to meet the competition offered by other national ECAs and thus "level the playing field" for all exporters. The main rationale for official export credit agencies is, of course, to facilitate the expansion of a country's exports and foreign exchange earnings based on comparative advantages of the country, by improving access to financing for exporters and encouraging banks to make that financing available on reasonable terms.

The specific rationale behind pre-shipment (working capital) guarantee programs is to encourage banks to lend to exporters, particularly newer and smaller firms and those with new products and markets, which are unable to provide adequate collateral or lack a sufficiently long record of successful operations. The ECA's pre-shipment guarantee helps to off-set banks' perceptions that lending to small enterprises, particularly those dependent on foreign sales, is excessively risky. It reduces banks' biases in favor of lending to large, domestically oriented firms. The pre-shipment guarantee should also reduce the banks' expenses of loan proc-essing—to the extent that they rely on the ECA's credit judgments and as a consequence do less work in credit investigation, loan collaterali-zation, and so on.[1]

The need for post-shipment export financing arises when exporters extend credit to their foreign buyers, since exporters, in order to be com-petitive, often must sell on credit terms. While much of the trade in commodities and consumer goods is sold on sight letter of credit or cash terms, foreign buyers often demand and receive credit terms of up to 180 days (and exceptionally up to 360 days). For capital equipment sales, medium- or long-term credit is often necessary, depending on the type and value of the equipment. As a result of the need to extend credit, exporters often require access to financing because they do not have sufficient resources to wait for payment from the foreign buyer.

The rationale behind all ECA post-shipment guarantee and insurance programs is to mitigate the risks of selling abroad on credit terms and thus encourage companies to expand their export sales. In addition to commercial risks such as delayed payment, default, insolvency, and bankruptcy, export credit sales involve significant political risks, which are beyond the control of both buyer and seller. Such political risks in-volve war, riot, revolution, expropriation, shortage of foreign exchange, and other transfer problems, which may impede payment after shipment of the goods to the buyer's country. Another category of political risk is the failure of a public buyer to repay its export credit, for whatever reason. Since public buyers are owned by governments, all risks of non-payment are classified as political. The commercial and political risks enumerated here are typically covered by export credit insurance. The cancellation of export or import licenses is also often part of standard political risk coverage, although it occurs in the pre-shipment period.

As noted, export credit insurance not only reduces the risk to the ex-porter, but can provide an incentive to commercial banks to finance the export transaction. Because the transaction is insured and the proceeds of the insurance policy can be assigned to the bank, the commercial bank can be assured of repayment from the proceeds of the export sale rather than depending only on the financial capacity of the exporter as security. Thus, exporters who obtain credit insurance potentially have access to greater resources from commercial banking sources.

Reducing the risk associated with financing export transactions to en-courage commercial bank lending is a major rationale for export credit guarantees. In such cases, the official agency issues a guarantee directly to the commercial bank that protects the bank from loss on its export credit, regardless of whether the loss was caused by action of the exporter or the foreign buyer. In the event that the loss was caused by the exporter, the official scheme will pay the bank and then proceed against the exporter for satisfaction of its claim. In developed countries, official guarantees are usually used for medium- and long-term transactions where banks are more concerned about risk than for short-term transactions. In developing countries where short-term financing is more limited, as noted earlier, official guarantees can provide a means for exporters to gain access to short-term export finance from commercial banks.

Export credit, guarantee and insurance programs are meant to provide exporters with improved access to export finance and to reduce individual firms' risks associated with extending credit to foreign buyers. Official export credit, guarantee and insurance programs also play a catalytic role in export development, alerting firms to the opportunities involved in export markets and how they can structure their sales to be internationally competitive. These programs also produce improved availability of credit information on countries and foreign buyers—something that is useful to both exporters and the commercial banking system. The expansion of export activity further familiarizes both bankers and exporters with financial risk and methods of reducing that risk, which is beneficial for general economic development.

The competitiveness argument—that national ECAs are needed to counter the effects of other national ECAs and level the playing field for exporters—tends to be a compelling argument for each national government. The U.S. government, for example, has frequently been motivated to go to great lengths through Eximbank (Export-Import Bank of the U.S.) to counter French export credit offers, there apparently being an atavistic rivalry between the two countries. However, critics note that from a broader perspective the competitiveness argument would fall apart if all nations agreed at the same time to eliminate, or at least limit, the programs of their official ECAs. This has been one of the major motivating factors behind international understandings to limit export credit terms, reached in the Organization for Economic Cooperation and Development (OECD) and the International Union of Credit and Investment Insurers (Berne Union).

The efficacy of ECAs as tools to stimulate additional exports is often questioned by critics, who say that it cannot be proved that the ECA caused the increase in exports that followed its inception and that export development is the result of many favorable policies and programs—not just ECAs. This is, of course, true. ECAs are a necessary but not sufficient (by themselves) tool for export development.

A study by First Washington Associates (FWA) of seventeen devel-

Table 5.1
The Relationship Between Official Export Finance Systems and the Growth of Manufactured Exports

Group	Pre-shipment export finance system	Average annual compound growth rate of mean manufactured export value 1974-86 (%)
Group 1	Available (A)	10.0
($0-27 million	Not available (N)	3.7
in exports)	A/N	2.7
Group 2	Available (A)	10.4
($28-59 million	Not available (N)	5.8
in exports)	A/N	1.8
Group 3	Available (A)	7.3
($60-337 million	Not available (N)	5.3
in exports)	A/N	1.4
Group 4	Available (A)	13.0
($338-2,534 million	Not available (N)	19.0
in exports)	A/N	0.7
Group 5	Available (A)	15.7
($2,535-30,723 million	Not available (N)	----
in exports)	A/N	----
Total	Available (A)	15.1
	Not Available (N)	6.8
	A/N	2.2

Source: The World Bank.

oping countries showed a cumulative increase of exports of $15.8 billion ten years prior to start-up of an ECA and $62.7 billion for the ten years after ECA start-up. The growth rates were 224 percent before the ECA and 331 percent after the ECA.[2] This indicates a clear linkage between ECAs and accelerating export development but cannot by itself prove that the former caused the latter.

In like fashion, the World Bank studied the relationship between establishment of pre-shipment guarantee programs and growth rate of exports.[3] They found that export growth rates for developing countries with pre-shipment guarantees were an average of 2.2 times greater than countries without these programs. The sole exception was the so-called Group 4 countries, which were among the two groups already having the highest level of national exports (see Table 5.1).

The rationales for establishing and supporting export credit agencies depend heavily upon other elements in a country's economy and the strength and sophistication of its exporters, banks, and other financial institutions. There is strong evidence that ECA programs increase exports with resultant economic and social benefits. However, a strict relationship between ECA activity and increased exports is hard to formulate because of numerous other variables affecting export success. Most experts agree that ECAs are necessary to maximize export possibilities in a competitive world but that ECAs by themselves cannot assure export success.

NOTES

1. Jacob Levitsky, *Best Practice in Credit Guarantees Schemes*. (Washington, DC: Inter-American Development Bank, 1995), 1.

2. First Washington Associates, *A Study of Institution Building for Post-Shipment Financing, Export Credit Insurance, and Guarantees in Developing Countries* (Arlington, VA: FWA, 1986), 22.

3. Yung Whee Rhee, *Trade Finance in Developing Countries* (Washington, DC: World Bank, 1989), 24.

6

History of ECAs

The first export credit insurance programs in the world were offered by Federal of Switzerland starting in 1906.[1] Federal is a privately owned company still operating today. The first government export credit insurance programs were established in the United Kingdom thirteen years later in 1919. The rationale for the British programs, which were eventually copied by other countries, was "to aid unemployment and to re-establish export trade disrupted by the conditions of war." In addition to export credit insurance, the British government established a trade finance program, offering up to six-year financing of exports at a preferential rate (1 percent above the Bank of England rate or a minimum of 8 percent). The British programs were administered by the Board of Trade with the consent of the Treasury, with the provision that income should be sufficient to meet possible losses.

As the Swiss and British programs proved themselves, other nations realized the efficacy and need for this type of government stimulation of trade. Accordingly, several other European countries established guarantee and insurance schemes, including Belgium (1921), Denmark (1922), the Netherlands (1923), Finland (1925), Germany (1926), Austria and Italy (1927), France and Spain (1928), and Norway (1929). The major rationale for establishing these programs was to re-establish export trade and revitalize industries devastated by World War I and to facilitate exports to the Soviet Union, a country that posed special risk factors to Western European business and that needed credit.

With the onset of worldwide economic depression after 1929, a new impetus was given to the establishment of official export credit, guarantee, and insurance facilities as a method of keeping up flows of trade and thus maintaining employment and output. During the 1930s, the following countries established such programs: Japan (1930); Czechoslovakia, Latvia, and Poland (1931); Sweden (1933); the United States (1934); and Ireland (1935). It is noteworthy that the United States had only official direct credit programs and not guarantee and insurance facilities in the first thirty years of operation of its Export-Import Bank (Eximbank). The other countries concentrated heavily on guarantees and insurance, with back-up discount lending to commercial banks to reduce interest rates. In 1934, a new international organization, the Berne Union (International Union of Credit and Investment Insurers), was established to encourage cooperation among national export credit insurers; to exchange information on buyers, countries, and technical matters; and to improve the level of competence of member countries.

By the mid-1930s, most export credit agencies (ECAs) were granting the majority of their insured credits to the Soviet Union, and despite the Depression, export credit insurance had proved very profitable. Most of the ECAs at that time were owned and operated entirely by governments.. However, four could be classified as "semiprivate" (Czechoslovakia, Germany, Netherlands, and Spain) and were operated by private firms with government financial and administrative assistance.

A major event of 1937 was the establishment of Banco Mexicano de Comercio Exterior (BANCOMEXT) in Mexico—the first ECA to be set up in a developing country. It concentrated on financing trade with North America and Europe in its early years and provided an example of official support, which was subsequently followed by many other Latin American countries.

The outbreak of World War II put a halt to the development of new export credit, guarantee, and insurance agencies from 1939 to 1945. Existing agencies turned their attention to financing activities that would help win the war. In the United States, for example, Eximbank financed exports that would help develop the rubber industry of Brazil and the mining industries of other Latin American countries whose outputs were vital for the war effort. The Burma Road to China was financed by the U.S. Eximbank, along with other projects that would contribute to military success.

At the end of World War II, the former Axis powers were confronted not only with rebuilding domestic economies but also with restoring their foreign trade. In the late 1940s and early 1950s, Japan established a full range of new insurance and financing programs as an essential aid to restoring exports and assisting in postwar reconstruction. Germany, Italy, and Austria also established new credit, guarantee, and insurance programs in the same time frame and for the same reasons.

In the latter half of the 1950s, significant further developments were realized. In 1956, South Africa established the first African export credit insurance program. In 1957, the Export Risks Insurance Corporation, a privately owned entity that was later replaced by a state-owned scheme, was established in India. Then in 1959, Morocco approved its own credit insurance program as a department of the Banque Marocaine du Commerce Exterieur.

These actions were followed by the establishment during the 1960s of a number of developing country export credit, guarantee, and insurance programs in Argentina, Bolivia, Brazil, Greece, Hong Kong, Korea, Pakistan, Peru, and Portugal. In all these cases, programs were intended to expand business activity and employment, improve international competitiveness, increase exports, and strengthen the balance of payments.

The third wave of developing countries to establish such programs occurred during the 1970s and included Ecuador, Jamaica, Malaysia, the Philippines, Singapore, Sri Lanka, Taiwan, Uruguay, and Venezuela. Increasingly, the motives for introducing export credit, guarantee, and insurance schemes seemed to include an awareness that the failure to do so would place the country at a severe competitive disadvantage, not only with regard to the OECD countries, but also in relation to other developing nations.

The 1980s saw a new group of countries enter into export credit, guarantee, and insurance activity, including Egypt, Indonesia, Tunisia, and Turkey.[2] Many of the schemes adopted in earlier years were changed in form and substance during this decade, the general trend being the establishment of organizations with more autonomy, a broader range of functions, and greater financial resources. In several cases, different export credit, guarantee, and insurance organizations were merged into one entity.

The 1990s witnessed the greatest growth of all in the establishment of official ECAs. Throughout Central and Eastern Europe and the former Soviet Union, new agencies were formed in the Czech Republic, Hungary, Lithuania, Poland, Russia, Slovakia, and Slovenia. In Kazakhstan, Ukraine, and other countries, foreign trade banks were reconfigured to offer standard ECA programs. In Latin America, several countries reconfigured their export finance agencies, including Brazil, Colombia, and Venezuela, and Chile opened its doors to a foreign-owned private sector export credit insurance company. In Africa, a regional export-import bank was formed to help and encourage the development of national ECAs, and in Asia, both China and Thailand formed export-import banks to consolidate and strengthen their dynamic export growth industries.

Throughout the 1980s, most OECD countries experienced heavy operational losses in their export credit, guarantee, and insurance programs. These losses were caused partly by the growing disparity between borrowing rates to fund the programs and the rates at which the funds were lent to finance exports. At the same time, nonpayment of officially supported export loans reached unprecedented magnitudes, as a result of developing country debt problems, defaults, and reschedulings. It was only in the 1990s that most industrial country ECAs returned to profitability as the Third World debt crisis gradually abated, fees and underwriting policies were adjusted, and export credit interest rates were raised to market levels.

Most industrial country ECAs have now been in operation for more than fifty years. More than half of the developing country ECAs have been in business for at least a decade and thus can be considered fully experienced in the appraisal and administration of export credit, guarantees, and insurance. The differences between industrial and developing countries in this field, which were tremendous in earlier years, are gradually narrowing and approaching common ground. The industrial countries have pulled back from overexpansion of credit to marginal markets, while the developing countries have sought to take more risk on credit sales without jeopardizing their financial soundness. Both developing and industrial countries have raised their interest rates to market-related levels and their common interest in avoiding a trade credit war has helped lead to greater harmonization of programs, policies, and procedures. With few exceptions, developing country ECAs have been profitable in recent years, and as a group, they have shown a substantial surplus. Industrial country ECAs have shown steady improvement in financial results during the 1990s, and in 1996, for the first time in seventeen years, they showed a profit as a group, with only a handful continuing to record losses. During the balance of the 1990s, most industrial country ECAs were profitable.

NOTES

1. International Union of Credit Insurers, *Collection of Histories of Members* (Paris, Berne Union, 1973).

2. Delio Gianturco, *Comprehensive Directory of the World's Export Credit Agencies* (Arlington, VA: First Washington Associates, 1991).

7

International Competitiveness

ECAs around the world generally try to ensure that their program offerings are internationally competitive; that is, that they place their
nations' firms on an equal footing with foreign exporters in the area of
export credit. There are various aspects to the international competitiveness of ECAs:

1. **Risk Assumption**:

   Willing to cover riskier markets
   Willing to cover riskier transactions
   Willing to provide high percentage of cover

2. **Underwriting Philosophy**:

   Aggressive approach to risk-taking
   Reasonable security requirements
   Maximum delegation of authority to others

3. **Program Accessibility**:

   Clarity of standards
   Consistency of standards
   Flexibility in deviating from standards

4. **Repayment term**:

   Willing to cover short (up to 1 year)
   Willing to cover medium (1–5 years)
   Willing to cover long (5–10 years)

5. Cost:

Reasonable level of insurance premiums and guarantee fees
Competitive, market-based interest rates
Acceptable types and levels of other charges

6. Eligible Buyers:

Broadest possible spread of countries
Broadest possible spread of buyers
Imaginative approach to acceptable security

7. Administrative Ease:

Simplicity of paperwork
Shortest possible processing of applications
Streamlined administration of outstanding commitments

8. Types of Coverage:

Both goods and services coverage
Pre-shipment and post-shipment coverage
Foreign direct investment coverage

9. Special Support:

Foreign content support
Flexible foreign currencies coverage
Feasibility study coverage, etc.

10. Guarantees to Banks:

Pre-shipment Guarantees
Post-shipment Guarantees
Delegated authority where possible

The Export-Import Bank of the U.S. (Eximbank) is required to make an annual report to the U.S. Congress on its competitiveness vs. other major ECAs.[1] In one of these reports, Eximbank noted its opinion that the main elements of competitiveness, in order of importance, were the level of fees, risk assumption, accessibility of programs, administrative ease, repayment terms, and extraordinary support. ECAs around the world attempt to maximize their competitiveness in each of these areas, bearing in mind that there are costs associated with all attempts to make their facilities more attractive to the export community and that they must maintain profitability and soundness of operations if they are to continue in business over the long run.

The level of ECA fees and length of repayment terms have been the easiest elements of competitiveness for analysts to measure and monitor. These two elements have been the primary focus of industrial country efforts to limit competition between official ECAs, thus reducing or eliminating subsidies connected with export credit. During the late 1960s and 1970s particularly, many official ECAs attempted to improve their competitiveness by extending repayment terms and lowering interest rates, often below their own cost of borrowing money. The result was growing red ink for the ECAs and an increasing sense that only the borrowers, not the ECA lenders, were benefiting from this situation. Accordingly, governments of the Organization for Economic Cooperation and Development (OECD) signed the Export Credit Arrangement explained elsewhere in this text. This OECD agreement places limits on minimum interest rates and on maximum repayment terms of standard export credits, therefore largely removing them as elements of inter-ECA competition.

Risk assumption, accessibility of programs, and administrative ease of working with an ECA are harder to assess as elements of competitiveness. An approach to objective evaluation of political risk assumption is explained in Chapter 20, where ECA country risk rating systems are discussed. However, there is no accepted methodology for measuring commercial risk assumption, accessibility of programs, or administrative ease. The competitiveness of these elements is usually judged subjectively, based on anecdotal evidence from users and/or the results of polls conducted by the ECAs with exporters and banks.

The last measure of competitiveness, extraordinary support, has mainly involved the use of tied aid or mixed credits. For such cases, overseas development agency (ODA) grants or long-term credits at concessional rates may be mixed with standard export credits to produce an exceptionally long average repayment term and low average interest rate on export-related financing, which is very attractive to foreign buyers. Limits have been placed on this practice by the OECD, but it remains a potent competitive tool in the hands of a few industrial country ECAs, mainly Japan, Spain, Denmark, France, Germany, Austria, Netherlands, and Belgium.

NOTE

1. United States Eximbank, *Report to the U.S. Congress on Export Credit Competition* (Washington, DC: U.S. Eximbank, 1999), p. 51.

8

International Co-operation

As mentioned in the previous chapter, export credit agencies (ECAs) are usually rivals, competing to finance their countries' exports in foreign markets. However, they are also partners when they cofinance products or projects involving exports from more than one country. Because of widespread recognition of the potential dangers and adverse effects of a trade credit war, ECAs have increasingly sought to foster international cooperation, coordinating their policies and practices on major issues and exchanging information between themselves that will be mutually beneficial. Two global associations (Berne Union and ICIA) and an intergovernmental organization (the OECD) now seek to harmonize ECAs' activities, exchange information, and adopt positions that will help all members to operate successfully. In addition, the World Bank, certain groups of countries, and individual national governments have undertaken major efforts to work together in the area of export credits, guarantees, and insurance.

THE BERNE UNION

In 1934, the international Union of Credit and Investment Insurers (Berne Union) was established, with the purpose of promoting the adoption of appropriate terms and conditions for export credit and foreign investment insurance and exchanging information between members that will help them to achieve operational success.[1] In its early years, the Berne Union limited its membership to industrial country ECAs, but this

Table 8.1
Members of the Berne Union

Argentina	(CASC)	Italy	(SACE)	Switzerland	(ERG)
Australia	(EFIC)	Italy	(EULER-SIAC)	Switzerland	(FEDERAL)
Austria	(OeKB)	Jamaica	(EXIMJ)	ChineseTaipei	(TEBC)
Belgium	(OND)	Japan	(EID/MITI)	Turkey	(TURKEXIMBANK)
Canada	(EDC)	Rep. Of Korea	(KEIC)	United Kingdom	(ECGD)
China	(PICC)	Malaysia	(MECIB)	United Kingdom	(ETI)
Cyprus	(ECIS)	Mexico	(BANCOMEXT)	United States	(EXIMBANK)
Czech Rep.	(EGAP)	Netherlands	(NCM)	United States	(FCIA)
Denmark	(EKF)	New Zealand	(EXGO)	United States	(OPIC)
Finland	(FINNVERA)	Norway	(GIEK)	Zimbabwe	(CREDSURE)
France	(COFACE)	Poland	(KUKE)	International Organization:	
Germany	(HERMES)	Portugal	(COSEC)	MIGA (World Bank Group)	
Germany	(C & L)	Singapore	(ECICS)		
Hong Kong	(HKEC)	South Africa	(CGIC)		
Hungary	(MEHIB)	Spain	(CESCE)		
India	(ECGC)	Spain	(CESSC)		
Indonesia	(ASEI)	Sri Lanka	(SLECIC)		
Israel	(IFTRIC)	Sweden	(EKN)		

Source: Berne Union.

changed radically in the 1970s and 1980s when many developing country ECAs sought and achieved membership, and the Berne Union is now open to ECAs around the world provided they meet minimum experience and activity level criteria. At the end of 1999, the Berne Union had a total of forty-eight members from forty countries and locations (see Table 8.1). The Berne Union Secretariat, now located in London, has also established co-operation arrangements with new export credit agencies in the Slovak Republic, Slovenia, Romania, Latvia, Russia and Uzbekistan.

The key role of the Berne Union ECAs is shown by the fact that in 1999 alone they supported exports of over $400 billion. In the preceding fifteen years, they covered almost $6 trillion of exports. This represented about half of the exports supported by all of the world's ECAs. The statutes of the union stipulate that its purpose shall be to work for the following:

1. The international acceptance of sound principles of export credit insurance and the establishment and maintenance of discipline in terms of credit for international trade.

2. International co-operation in encouraging a favorable investment climate and in developing and maintaining sound principles of foreign investment insurance.

3. The exchange of information, assistance, expertise and advice in relation to the commercial and political risks involved in export credit insurance, to the political risks involved in foreign investment insurance and to the range of associated matters relating thereto.

To achieve these aims, Berne Union members agree that they will do the following:

1. exchange information and furnish the union with the information necessary for the accomplishment of its tasks.
2. maintain and adhere to the maximum credit terms and starting points of credit set out in a series of agreements and understandings.
3. consult together on a continuing basis, carry out studies, and participate in agreed projects.
4. co-operate closely and, where appropriate, take co-ordinated action.
5. co-operate with other international institutions concerned.

Members of the Berne Union meet together at least twice a year, and each year there is also at least one workshop (sometimes attended by nonmembers as observers) and one specialist workshop. Bilateral exchanges of information occur hundreds of times daily among Berne Union members, since one of the obligations of membership is to respond to other members' requests for information on terms, creditworthiness, and other aspects of individual buyer transactions. Technically, the Berne Union is an organization of companies, not governments. Even though many of the companies are government-owned, the members take positions that are binding on the ECA, but not on the parent government. Despite this technicality, governments have unofficially recognized that Berne Union understandings should be supported. The Berne Union is the international organization most concerned with short-term export credit issues.

THE INTERNATIONAL CREDIT INSURANCE ASSOCIATION

The International Credit Insurance Association (ICIA) was constituted under Swiss law in 1928 and is presently domiciled in London. Unlike the Berne Union, all of the ICIA's members are private sector companies. Its object is "to study questions relating to credit and guarantee insurance, to provide opportunities for members' employees to acquire knowledge of the theory and practice of credit insurance and guarantee underwriting and to initiate means whereby the common action of the members can be facilitated in order to develop their mutual relations in the interest of their national and the international economy, in the interest of their insured and in their own interest."[2] As of January 2000, the ICIA had forty-five members from twenty-seven countries (see Table 8.2). Most, but not all, of the forty-five ICIA members offer export credit insurance. Other financial programs offered by members include domestic credit insurance, lines of guarantee, and surety bonds. It is estimated that ICIA members together covered trade credit—through both domes-

Table 8.2
Members of the ICIA

Argentina	Aseguradora de Créditos y Garantias S.A.
Australia	QBE Trade Indemnity Limited
Austria	Österreichische Kreditversicherungs-Aktiengesellschaft
	Prisma Kreditversicherungs-Aktiengesellschaft
Belgium	Euler-Cobac S.A.
	Gerling Namur - Assurances du Credit S.A.
Canada	The Guarantee Company of North America
Demark	Dansk Kautionsforsikrings-Aktieselskab
Finland	Pohjola Nonlife Insurance Company Ltd.
France	Compagnie Francaise d'Assurance pour Le Commerce Extérieur (COFACE)
	Euler-Société Francaise d'Assurance Crédit (SFAC)
Germany	Allgemeine Kreditversicherung Aktiengesellschaft
	Gerling Speziale Kreditversicherungs-AG
	Hermes Kreditversicherungs-Aktiengesellschaft
Greece	The "Ethniki" - Hellenic General Insurance Company S.A.
Ireland	Church and General Corporate Insurance p.l.c.
Israel	Clal Credit Insurance Limited
Italy	Concordato Cauzione Credito 1994
	Euler-SIAC Societa Italiana Assicurazione Crediti Spa
	Societa Italiana Cauzioni
Japan	Mitsui Marine & Fire Insurance Co. Ltd.
	The Tokio Marine & Fire Insurance Co. Ltd.
	The Yasuda Fire & Marine Insurance Co. Ltd.
Korea	Seoul Guarantee Insurance Company
Mexico	Fianzas Atlas S.A.
	Compania Mexicana de Sequros de Crédito S.A.
Netherlands	N.V. Nationale Borg-Maatschappij N.V.
Norway	Gerling - Nordic Kredittofrsikring A.S.
Philippines	Malayan Insurance Company Inc.
Poland	WARTA Insurance & Reinsurance Company Ltd.
Portugal	COSEC - Companhia de Seguro de Créditos S.A.
Singapore	ECICS Credit Insurance Ltd.
South Africa	Credit Guarantee Insurance Corporation of Africa Ltd.
Spain	CESCC-Compania Espanola de Seguros-y Reaseguros de Crédito y Caucion,S.A.
	CESCE - Compania Espanola de Seguros de Crédito a la Exportacion, S.A.
	Mapfre Caucion y Credito Compañia Internacional de Seguros-y Reaseguros S.A.
Switzerland	Eidgenössische Versicherungs-Aktien-Gesellschaft
U.K.	Euler Trade Indemnity Plc
	Zurich GSG Limited
U.S.	Chubb-Federal Insurance Company
	Euler American Credit Indemnity Company
	Fidelity & Deposit Company of Maryland
	The St. Paul Surety
	Travelers Casualty and Surety Company

tic and export credit insurance—in excess of $1 trillion in 1999. Together with the Berne Union, the ICIA is sponsoring the establishment of an International Institute of Professional Credit & Surety Underwriters, which was scheduled to begin operations in 2001. The institute will operate a distance learning program, including the offer of a three-year diploma in credit insurance.

ORGANIZATION FOR ECONOMIC CO-OPERATION AND DEVELOPMENT

The Organization for Economic Co-operation and Development (OECD) is the other international group that seeks to organize and regulate export credit. The OECD, headquartered in Paris, is an organization whose members are the governments of the industrial countries. The OECD has an Export Credits Group, which meets regularly to exchange information on financing extended by member countries.

The most significant result of the OECD's work has been the conclusion of the Arrangement on Officially Supported Export Credits, which places limitations on the percentage of an export that is financed, the term of financing, and the interest rates offered.[3] It also regulates other terms and conditions of medium- and long-term export credits and imposes some restrictions on "tied aid" or "mixed credits." All of the OECD countries have subscribed to this arrangement, which is of interest to the developing countries because it prescribes the maximum terms they will normally receive on export credits and also gives the developing countries a fairly clear idea of the maximum terms they may have to support when they are extending export credits to other countries in competition with OECD suppliers.

Key sections of the OECD Arrangement on Officially Supported Export Credits are shown in Appendix B. This agreement is reviewed semiannually. The arrangement covers officially supported export credits with a maturity of two years and longer except for military exports and agricultural commodities exports. It imposes a minimum cash payment requirement of 15 percent and maximum financing of 85 percent of export value. Repayment terms cannot exceed five years for relatively rich countries, but 8.5 years may be granted with prior notification to other members and 10 years for relatively poor countries. Officially supported interest rates are expected to correspond to market rates (called CIRRS) and to be free of subsidy.

The OECD arrangement imposes special provisions for tied aid or mixed credits (which includes loans, grants, or associated financing packages for exports that have a concessionality level greater than 80 percent). "Concessionality level" is defined as the difference between the nominal value of the loan and the discounted present value of the future debt service payments, expressed as a percentage of the nominal value of the loan. Tied aid is prohibited to developing countries that have a relatively high per capita income (using 1995 data, those with over $3,035 GNP per capita). Tied aid is also prohibited if it has a concessionality level of less than 35 percent (or 50 percent for certain countries). All tied aid credits are supposed to be notified by the originating ECA to all other OECD ECAs. The reduction in these credits since 1992 is noteworthy (see Table 8.3).

In 1998, the OECD members agreed to a new aspect of the arrange-

Table 8.3
Tied Aid Offers (1991–1998) (in billion US$)

YEAR	TIED AID
1991	9
1992	10
1993	4
1994	5
1995	4
1996	4
1997	3
1998	4
1999	5

ment: minimum guarantee and insurance premiums. These premiums or exposure fees are divided into seven-country risk categories and vary with the percentage of cover offered. The intention behind the premium agreement is to eliminate this aspect of ECA operations as a potential form of subsidy (i.e., if premiums were intentionally insufficient to cover related claims). The new OECD premium agreement is in Appendix C.

INTERNATIONAL TRADE CENTER

The International Trade Center (ITC) used to provide a limited amount of technical assistance to developing countries to help them establish export credit and guarantee and insurance programs. The ITC is a venture originally sponsored by General Agreement on Tariffs and Trade (GATT) and the United Nations Council on Trade and Development (UNCTAD) and is headquartered in Geneva, Switzerland. Established in 1973 as the focal point for U.N. assistance in trade promotion, the ITC provided consultancy services, seminars, and symposia on export financing to developing countries until about 1990. Funding limitations and a shortage of staff prevented the ITC from playing a larger role. However, in some cases, its assistance served as a catalyst to focus other attention and resources on the export credit area and, thus, helped produce changes that are supportive of general export expansion. In the late 1990s, the ITC limited its ECA program mainly to sponsorship of publications and conferences on trade finance, oriented heavily to the transition economies of Central and Eastern Europe and the former Soviet Union.

MULTILATERAL INVESTMENT GUARANTEE AGENCY

The Multilateral Investment Guarantee Agency (MIGA) was established in April 1988 as part of the World Bank Group, in order to "encourage the flow of investments for productive purposes among member countries."[4] To achieve this objective, MIGA "issues guarantees, including coinsurance and reinsurance, against non-commercial risks in respect of investments in a member country which flow from other member countries." To conserve scarce resources and avoid duplication with ECAs, MIGA has followed a policy of not guaranteeing or reinsuring any export credit, regardless of its form, which is provided, guaranteed, or reinsured by a government or an official ECA. "[However] exports will be covered (within the limits of the preceding sentence) . . . to the extent that they represent a contribution to a specific investment." By late 1999, MIGA had 149 member countries owning its authorized capital of $1 billion, with another 16 countries in the process of fulfilling membership requirements. MIGA is now an active issuer of political risk guarantees to foreign investors in its developing member countries, providing coverage against transfer restriction, expropriation, war, and civil disturbance. MIGA works with ECAs around the world, sharing technical knowledge, providing coverage to investors who want political risk insurance for investments in other countries, and providing co-insurance for some ECAs who are willing to participate in the basic political risk insurance coverage.

EUROPEAN REGIONAL APPROACHES

The European Union (EU) sponsors periodic meetings of the ECAs of member countries in order to harmonize policies, facilitate intraregional trade, adopt common approaches to external trade, and agree on positions to be taken in international discussions and agreements. In the early 1990s, EU PHARE, the EU's aid agency, provided a substantial amount of funding for technical assistance and training to Central and Eastern European (CEE) export credit, guarantee, and insurance programs. Its programs were also made available to countries in the former Soviet Union. Another European initiative to help trade finance has been that of the European Bank for Reconstruction and Development (EBRD), which has funded technical assistance for the Export-Import Bank of Uzbekistan and has provided trade guarantees for several CEE countries and Russia.

Since the mid-1990s the European Union countries have adhered to an understanding that they will no longer support export credit insurance for "marketable" risks (defined as short-term commercial risks pertaining to sales with most OECD countries) by providing any of the following: "state guarantees for borrowing or losses; exemption from the requirement to constitute adequate reserves and other requirements; relief or exemption from taxes or other charges normally payable; award of aid or provisions of capital or other forms of finance in circumstances in which a private investor acting under normal market conditions would not invest in the company or on terms a private investor would not accept; provision by the state of services in kind, such as access to and use of state infrastructure, facilities or privileged information (for instance, information about debtors gathered by embassies), on terms not reflecting their cost; and reinsurance by the state, either directly, or indirectly via a public or publicly supported export insurer, on terms more favorable than those available from the private reinsurance market, which leads either to under-underpricing of the reinsurance cover or in the artificial creation of capacity that would not be forthcoming from the private market."[5] This prohibition has resulted in a great stimulus to the operation of privately owned export credit insurers.

AFRICAN REGIONAL APPROACHES

The Dakar Union is an informal grouping of ten African and two Caribbean countries, which was set up in 1984 to encourage and improve export credit insurance and financing activity, assist in the exchange of information between members, and help countries that did not have export credit insurance programs to set them up. Members consist of both ECAs and export promotion organizations. In the 1990s, the Dakar Union was relatively inactive.

The major African regional initiative for ECAs in the last decade has been establishment of the African Export-Import Bank (AFREXIM). Sponsored by the African Development Bank, AFREXIM is expected to play a major role in ECA developments on that continent. A more complete examination of AFREXIM is contained in chapter 13.

LATIN AMERICAN REGIONAL APPROACHES

The Asociacion Latinoamericana de Seguradoras de Credito a la Exportacion (ALASECE) was formed in 1982 with the objective of developing cooperation between Latin American and Caribbean export credit insurers, broadening and strengthening their activities, and improving their internal operations and external mechanisms for financing exports.[6] ALASECE allows full membership by export credit and promotion agencies, organizations that promote regional integration, and export credit insurers from outside the region. ALASECE is primarily interested in facilitating exchanges of technical information between members, serving as a conduit for the extension of technical assistance to improve national export credit insurance and finance capabilities, and encouraging joint operations and cooperation between member countries and institutions. The organization also seeks to harmonize financing systems and credit terms, and to promote the services to their export communities. ALASECE's membership as of January 1998 is shown in Table 8.4.

The Inter-American Development Bank, BLADEX, Andean Development Corporation, Central American Bank for Economic Integration, and

Table 8.4
ALASECE Membership, January 1998

Active Members

Aseguradora de Créditos y Garantias S.A.	Argentina
COFACE	Chile
Compañia Argentina de Seguros de Crédito a la Exportación S.A.	Argentina
Compañia Mexicana de Seguros de Crédito S.A.	Mexico
Cia de Seguros de Crédito Continental S.A.	Chile
Instituto de Resseguros do Brasil	Brazil
La Mundial C.A. Venezolana de Seguros de Crédito S.A.	Venezuela
Mapfre Garantías y Crédito S.A.	Chile
Secrex Compañia de Seguros de Créditos y Garantias S.A.	Peru
Sequrexpo de Colombia S.A.	Colombia
Aseguradora de Crédito y del Comercio Exterior	Colombia
Cuba S.A. ESICUBA	Cuba
Trinidad & Tobago Export Credit Insurance Company, Ltd.	Trinidad/Tobago

Adherent Members

Banco de Inversión y Comercio Exterior, BICE	Argentina
COFACE	France
Banco Nacional de Comercio Exterior	Mexico
Compañia Española de Seguros de Crédito a la Exportación	Spain
Münchener Rück	Germany
SCOR Reassurance	France

Organization for Eastern Caribbean States all offer regional and subregional trade financing programs for Latin American and Caribbean exporters. Descriptions of those facilities are in chapter 13.

ASIAN REGIONAL APPROACHES

The U.N. Conference on Trade and Development, other U.N. agencies, and the Asian Development Bank (ADB) have considered the possibilities of establishing regional trade finance programs from time to time. However, no action had been taken on any of these proposals by the year 2000. The ADB has provided a small amount of financing for technical assistance to help individual national ECAs, but this was not a special focus of the ADB's lending until early 1998. At that time, the ADB approved a $1 billion trade finance facility for Thailand to be administered by the country's export-import bank. In 1999, the ADB approved a $300 million loan to improve Pakistan's export finance system, and further commitments of this nature are anticipated in coming years.

THE WORLD BANK

The World Bank has played a major role in the development of a number of countries' export credit, guarantee, and insurance facilities.

Export Development Fund (EDF) lending was an early part of the bank's response to the pressing needs of member countries for assistance in the export credit, guarantee, and insurance area.[7] EDF lending began in 1979 and was especially oriented to meeting the short-term foreign exchange working capital needs of exporters. The World Bank's EDF loans involved "(i) providing resources to a self-sustaining revolving fund administered by an ECA that allowed exporters to import inputs needed for export production; and (ii) supporting policy and administrative reforms required for increased international competitiveness and more efficient trade performance."[8] EDF-supported loans to exporters paid for essential imported raw materials, parts and components incorporated in export products, carried a market-related rate of interest, and a repayment term to exporters not exceeding one year (which might include thirty to ninety days to permit the exporter to receive payment from a foreign buyer).

Another form of World Bank assistance to export credit, guarantee, and insurance entities in recent years has been the provision of technical assistance (TA) funding to assist in the design and start-up of new organizations and programs and to improve the capabilities of existing institutions. At least two dozen countries have utilized TA funding for this purpose. The bank has also carried out a number of missions that have examined the policies, programs, and effectiveness of export, guarantee and insurance programs in member countries and have produced reports recommending changes which would enhance their contribution to overall export development.

In 1985, the World Bank took another major step forward in the export credit, guarantee, and insurance area with the approval of a $100 million loan to assist in establishing the Export Development Bank of Egypt. A similar loan was made to Turkey to establish its export credit bank about five years later. In the 1990s, the World Bank instituted other programs which helped in ECA development. For instance, the IBRD approved special political risk guarantee programs for Albania, Moldova, Ukraine, and Bosnia-Herzegovina to cover goods imported by those countries, many of which were to be transformed into export products and sold abroad. Also in Ukraine, special financing was approved to convert a largely commercial bank into a new full-service export-import bank, using a "twinning arrangement" with the Export-Import Bank of Japan. In the twenty years from 1979 to 1999, the World Bank approved a total of over $2 billion of loans to improve export credit and trade finance agencies in developing and transition countries (see Table 8.5).

INTER-AMERICAN DEVELOPMENT BANK

The Inter-American Development Bank (IADB) has also had a long history of involvement in developing export finance programs for its mem-

Table 8.5
World Bank Projects Supporting ECA and Trade Finance Development

Fiscal Year	Country	Beneficiary	US$ Amount
1999	Turkey	Turk Eximbank	$253 million
1997	Albania	Albanian Guarantee Agency	$ 10 million
1996	Bosnia	IGA	$ 10 million
1994	Moldova	Guarantee Administration Unit, MOF	$ 30 million
1993	Argentina	BICE	$150 million
1993	Bulgaria	National Bank	$ 55 million
1993	Colombia	BANCOLDEX	$200 million
1993	Ghana	Ministry of Finance (IDA)	$ 41 million
1993	Romania	Various	$450 million
1987	Turkey	TEXIM	$250 million
1984	Egypt	Export Development Bank of Egypt	$275 million
1983	Mexico	BANCOMEXT	$275 million
1983	Jamaica	JECIC	$ 28 million
1983	Costa Rica	Export Development	$ 25 million
1983	Zimbabwe	Export Promotion	$ 70 million
1981	Jamaica	JECIC	$ 26 million
1981	Guyana	Central Bank	$ 8 million
1979	Jamaica	JECIC	$ 30 million
		Total	$2,186 million

Source: World Bank.

ber countries on both a regional and national basis. In the mid-1970s, for example, the IADB played a leading role in helping to establish the Banco Latino Americano de Exportaciones (BLADEX), an intraregional ECA. Earlier, in 1964, the IADB established an intraregional export finance facility to cover medium-term exports between Latin American countries.[9] The facility provided lines of credit to central banks for eligible export transactions. In 1975, the program was expanded to cover exports by member countries to destinations outside the region. In 1980, the IADB reduced the number of member countries eligible to use the program and imposed other limitations. During the early 1990s, the IADB export finance programs were only lightly utilized, and as of the year 2000, these programs had been effectively discontinued. In addition to financial programs, the IADB has sponsored seminars and training in ECA management for design and start-up of new facilities. An IADB representative regularly attends general meetings of the Berne Union.

BILATERAL ASSISTANCE

During the 1960s and 1970s, the export credit, guarantee, and insurance programs of a number of developing countries were assisted in their design and start-up phases by ECAs in industrial countries and, occasionally, by concessional assistance agencies. In the 1990s, several transition countries received similar bilateral assistance.

The help rendered by industrial countries' export credit, guarantee, and insurance agencies has usually taken two forms: short training sessions for developing country personnel within the industrial country ECA and, less frequently, the loan of an expert to the developing country for a brief period to help design or start up its programs. The concessional assistance agencies have usually gotten involved with ECAs in former colonies or when there were special geographical, political, or economic ties between the two countries. The major contribution of aid agencies to date has been in paying for technical assistance to help design and start up developing country programs (i.e., Scandinavian and Dutch aid to Central and Eastern Europe, and U.S. aid to Africa). Aid agencies have also contributed in a few instances to the reserves of developing countries' export credit, guarantee, and insurance agencies.

CO-FINANCING

A whole other area of international co-operation of ECAs involves co-financing with the multinational development banks (MDBs). When the MDBs work with ECAs, as opposed to other multilateral or bilateral sources of co-financing, the ECAs typically introduce markets and projects to private funding, which otherwise would not participate in a project. Successful co-financing between MDBs and ECAs increases the familiarity and willingness of the private sector to lend in the markets concerned. Also, ECAs view the MDB's involvement as a way to ensure that projects have been scrutinized carefully and that they fit the overall development strategy of the country. They also believe MDB participation improves the probability of prompt repayment. Co-financing between MDBs and ECAs as opposed to co-financing directly with private sources of capital has the advantage that the MDB does not guarantee payment to the ECAs. Thus, co-financing with ECAs minimizes the MDB's commitment of funds and maximizes its leverage.

Some ECAs criticize the MDBs for not making their guarantee available to them. Also, co-financing is seen by some ECAs as overly complex, difficult to arrange, and time-consuming. Despite this, MDBs have in fact made heavy use of the ECAs as co-financiers. Both the World Bank and the EBRD adopted new programs in the 1990s to obtain ECA co-financing and made special efforts to enlist ECA support for individual projects. The World Bank, for example, obtained 15 percent of all of its co-financing from ECAs in the decade from 1985 to 1995. The EBRD also obtained 15 percent of its co-financing from the ECAs between 1991 and 1995. World Bank/ECA co-financing operations in recent years demonstrate a wide diversity and scope (see Table 8.6).

Table 8.6
Export Credit Co-Financing by Region and Sector (Million US$, fiscal years)

	1990	1991	1992	1993	1994	1995	1971-1995	
							$ million	Per cent of total
Africa	17	147	1,174	10	-	-	2,054	8
East Asia & the Pacific	1,186	75	1,956	157	92	348	7,609	29
Middle East & North Africa	48	-	-	48	23	-	1,224	5
Latin America & the Caribbean	2,074	-	-	700	2	-	8,748	33
Europe & Central Asia	134	227	-	-	174	-	2,353	9
South Asia	60	746	207	289	300	50	4,256	16
Total	3,519	1,195	3,337	1,203	591	398	26,252	100
Agriculture	-	-	-	-	2	-	369	1
Telecommunications	131	45	109	-	149	178	1,941	7
Education	-	-	-	-	-	-	6	0
Financial	-	75	-	-	-	-	284	1
Energy	-	888	7	7	47	170	2,799	11
Population, health & nutrition	-	-	-	-	-	-	8	0
Industrial development finance	48	-	-	-	-	-	1,685	6
Mining & other extractive	-	-	-	-	-	-	938	4
Power	3,205	187	2,048	1,186	392	50	14,652	56
Tourism	-	-	-	-	-	-	10	0
Transportation	100	-	-	10	-	-	2,119	8
Urban	-	-	-	-	-	-	14	-
Water supply & Sanitation	34	-	1,174	-	-	-	427	5
Total	3,519	1,195	3,337	1,203	591	398	26,253	100

Note: These figures are based on the financing plans. Co-financing data are reported by the fiscal year in which the project is presented to the Board of the Bank. These figures include co-financing with bank loans and credits and projects financed by bank-managed trust funds. The number count in this table represents the number of projects.

It should be noted that the very large amount of co-financing provided under the united loan facility of the Export Import Bank of Japan is now technically reported under bilateral co-financing and therefore is not included in export credit figures.

Source: World Bank.

NOTES

1. International Union of Credit and Investment Insurers, *The Berne Union: Export Credit Insurance, Overseas Investment Insurance* (London Berne Union, 1988), p. 6.

2. International Credit Insurance Association, *1999/2000 Directory* (London ICIA, 1999), p. 2.

3. Organization for Economic Cooperation and Development, *The Export Credit Arrangement* (Paris: OECD Publications, 1998), 17.

4. World Bank, *Convention Establishing the Multilateral Investment Guarantee Agency* (Washington, DC: World Bank, 1985), p. 4.

5. European Commission, Communication Applying Articles 92 and 93 of the Treaty of Short-Term Export Credit Insurance, *Official Journal* C281 (Brussels, Belgium: EC, 1997), 4–5.

6. Asociacion Latinoamericana de Organismos de Seguro de Credito a la Exportacion, *Bulletin No. 2.* (Bogota, Colombia: ALASECE, 1996), 2.

7. World Bank, *World Bank Lending for Export Development Funds* (Washington, DC: World Bank, 1983), 1.

8. World Bank, *World Bank Lending for Export Development Funds* (Washington, DC. World Bank, 1983), 1.

9. Inter-American Development Bank, *Evaluation Review on the Promotion and Financing of Exports* (Washington, DC: IDB, 1993), 10.

9

Types of Organization

Many different types of organizations administer export credit, guarantee, and insurance programs in countries around the world. For the first half of the twentieth century, almost all ECAs were governmental organizations of one type or another. However, during the second half of the century, there were increasing numbers of private and mixed public/private organizations offering such programs. The present multiplicity of ECA organization types mainly reflects the extent of national government's willingness to participate, the types of programs that are being offered, and the actual and projected levels of activity of these programs.

The relationships between official export credit agencies (ECAs) and their governments are varied and often complex. In conducting officially supported export credit business, ECAs have differing levels of independence, and the extent of this independence appears to depend little on whether the agency is in the public or private sector. However, all ECAs that rely on financial support from governments are ultimately accountable to those governments, and most have "guardian authorities," which direct overall policies regarding official support and represent the ECAs in their intergovernmental relations.

The organizational entities that administer official export loan programs include (a) departments of central banks, (b) executive agencies for concessional aid programs for developing countries, (c) special funds established within a central bank or its subsidiary, (d) departments of export credit insurance corporations, (e) government-owned or mixed export credit institutions, (f) independent or semi-independent export-import banks, and (g) private banking consortiums.[1]

Organizational set-ups for export guarantees and insurance include (a) government departments or agencies, (b) insurance companies or banking institutions acting as agent for the government, (c) public corporations or public funds that are autonomous but wholly government owned, (d) companies that are jointly owned by government and private banks or insurance companies, and (e) privately owned insurance companies operating with government co-insurance or reinsurance.

A number of factors dictate the type of export credit agency that is best for a country, including (a) the willingness and ability of private sector interests (normally banks or insurance companies) to assume ownership, management, and risk-taking obligations in the new organization; (b) the availability of an existing governmental organization with the requisite interest, skills, authority and related activities to play a meaningful role; (c) organizational precedents established in the country by the government for similar activities; (d) legislative and statutory limitations and opportunities; (e) the actual relationship and degree of confidence existing between the government and the private sector; and (f) the relative ability of each type of organization to recruit, train, and retain the skilled personnel necessary to make the export credit guarantees and insurance successful.

The type of ECA organization selected by a country also seems to depend heavily on two factors: (1) geographic area of the world and (2) date of start-up. In Europe, the major ECA in each country tends to be an export credit insurance company with a separate export finance company or bank. Exceptions exist in many countries, of course, such as the United Kingdom (where the Export Credits Guarantee Department [ECGD], a government department, performs all services) and Austria (where the Oesterreichische Kontrollbank [OeKb], a government bank, also offers loans, guarantees, and insurance). In North America, the relatively autonomous, government-owned export-import bank (eximbank) or export finance corporation is the predominant organizational format. In Asia, Africa, and Latin America, there is significant organizational diversity, with the type of ECA being influenced by patterns in the metropolitan country.

An equally important influence on ECA type seems to be the time when the ECA was organized. After World War II, several Asian countries opted to establish eximbanks—apparently because of the success and prestige of the U.S. model at that time. Japan, Korea, and Taiwan all established eximbanks in the twenty years after 1945 and were very successful in using them to stimulate exports. Their examples have been widely followed by other countries.[2] In more recent times, China and Thailand have also established eximbanks, along with a diverse group of countries in Central and Eastern Europe, the former Soviet Union, Latin America, the Caribbean, and Africa. In fact, the eximbank form of organization has been adopted by the largest number of official ECAs established from 1980 onward, with second place going to the export credit insurance company.

The primary advantages that eximbanks often have over other forms of ECAs are as follows: (a) a convenient organizational format for soliciting private sector participation in ownership; (b) a large, defined capital base which can be used to support a high volume of activity; (c) operational autonomy which can result in private sector standards of employment and remuneration; (d) greater insulation from political pressures; (e) the ability to offer all kinds of financial support including loans, guarantees, and insurance; (f) a potentially greater ability to attract financial resources from abroad; and (g) as a result, a greater possibility of meeting total national export development needs, while operating in a businesslike fashion.

NOTES

1. First Washington Associates, *A Study of Institution Building for Post-Shipment Financing, Export Credit Insurance and Guarantees to Banks in Developing Countries* (Arlington, VA: FWA, 1986), 22.

2. United Nations Conference on Trade and Development, *A Prototype Model of a Trade-Finance Facility in Developing Countries: An Export-Import Bank* (Geneva, Switzerland: UNCTAD, 1996), 5.

10

Industrial Countries

Every industrial country has at least one official export credit agency (ECA). Many have two agencies: one for finance and one for guarantees and insurance. Sometimes, a third agency exists, just to offer pre-shipment working capital guarantees. In addition, many industrial countries now have at least one private export credit insurance company, offering competition to the official scheme mainly in the short-term area. Most of the official ECAs have been in business for at least fifty years. Thus, they have gone through many cycles, both good and bad, and have gained great expertise in export credit, guarantee, and insurance management.

Almost all of the industrial country ECAs were managed on more or less businesslike principles until the late 1960s when production capacity in the industrial countries expanded substantially and export credit competition became increasingly intense. As a consequence, the industrial ECAs began to reduce interest rates, lengthen repayment terms, and make loans to riskier customers in order to give their national exporters an advantage—even if only temporary—over their competition. At the same time, portfolio exposure limits were continually expanded and then, for some ECAs, ultimately discarded completely. The result was that by the end of the 1970s almost all industrial country ECAs were overextended, particularly with regard to their exposure in the developing countries, and their profit margins were badly eroded. Thus, they were ill equipped for the abrupt cessation of payments, first from Mexico and then from many other developing countries, which began in 1982 and lasted for almost a decade. The result was financial chaos, management disorientation, and waning public support for ECAs in the industrial countries throughout the 1980s.

About midway through this troubled period, most industrial country ECAs desisted from subsidizing their exports by the extension of low interest credits, stopped consciously covering transactions in countries offering small possibility of prompt payment, and started to charge risk premiums that were more adequate to cover probable defaults. Creditor governments had to fund substantial cash flow deficits as a consequence of former excesses, and they brought pressure to bear on the ECAs to reform their operations. At the same time, the ECAs and their guardian authorities reached new international agreements to restrict credit terms and raise interest rates to market levels.

Fortunately, as a result of gradually improving economic conditions, stimulated by massive support from the World Bank and the International Monetary Fund (IMF), the debtor countries slowly reduced their recourse to unilateral debt moratoria and Paris Club reschedulings. As a result, most industrial country ECAs were restored to profitability in the early 1990s. By the late 1990s, international negotiations were completed to raise industrial country ECAs' risk premiums to eliminate these as a source of subsidy.

Industrial country ECAs still differ widely in their approach to covering exports to individual countries. Some ECAs are criticized for excessive caution and others for not paying enough attention to underlying risks and effective methods of mitigating those risks. A "lemming effect" of supporting exports to weaker countries, solely because competitors are doing so, has been noted. Significant advances have been made in the area of co-financing with multilateral development banks. At the same time, project finance and securitized lending, which do not rely upon sovereign guarantees of borrowers' obligations, have been advanced in sophistication and frequency of utilization by industrial country ECAs.

As noted by the IMF, officially supported export credits have played a critical role in providing developing countries with short-, medium-, and long-term financing.[1] Industrial country ECAs often subject these credits to more rigorous evaluations than most commercial banks and have refined their country risk assessment systems to reinforce the linkage between new financing and appropriate debtor country policies and performance. Other trends include an increased ECA emphasis on financing by and for the private sector, improved project selection, and closer collaboration with other lenders.

It should be noted, however, that industrial country ECAs have a number of limitations on their usefulness as a device for transferring capital to the developing countries. The biggest limitation is that export credits

Table 10.1
Medium- and Long-Term Indebtedness of Developing Countries and Economies in Transition, 1995

| | In Billions of US$ | Shares in Percent | |
		In Total debt	In Official debt
Export Credits	$ 357	20.6%	37.0%
ODA	$ 146	8.4%	15.1%
Other bilateral	$ 188	10.9%	19.5%
Multilateral	$ 275	15.9%	28.5%
Total official	**$ 966**	**55.6%**	**100.0%**
Banks & other	$ 765	44.4%	
Of which: Short-term	$ 358	20.7%	
Total	**$1,731**	**100.0%**	

Sources: Organization for Economic Cooperation and Development (OECD) and International Monetary Fund (IMF).

are directly linked to sales of goods and services from their countries and thus cannot be expanded without underlying commercial transactions that are satisfactory to both sides. Secondly, most ECA financing is very short term in nature and thus can sometimes exacerbate, rather than work to solve, debt-servicing problems. Third, the interest rates payable on ECA credits are not concessionary. Fourth, when ECAs make long-term credits available, these are almost always related to major projects that have extended disbursement periods. ECA credits are then generally ineffective in addressing developing countries' immediate balance of payments problems and certainly less favorable in their terms and conditions than credits from the IMF, World Bank, and overseas development assistance agencies. Finally, export credits are generally unavailable for the poorest countries because of ECA requirements to find reasonable assurance of repayment.

The importance of industrial country ECAs as vehicles for transferring capital to developing countries is demonstrated by the fact that 20.6 percent of all developing and transition countries' indebtedness and 37.0 percent of all official debt was owed to ECAs as of the beginning of 1995 (see Table 10.1). This makes industrial country export credit agencies the largest single source of official capital for the rest of the world, eclipsing the contribution of overseas development agencies (ODA), other bilateral agencies, and multilateral organizations (the World Bank group, etc.).

Medium- and long-term ECA credits are heavily concentrated in Latin America, East Asia, and Pacific, followed closely by Europe and Central Asia, and the Middle East and North Africa. Sub-Saharan Africa and South Asia have received the least in ECA credit.

Table 10.2
Twenty Main Recipients of Exporting Credits Among Developing Countries and Countries in Transition, 1996 (in billions of US$)

Russia	52.9
China	44.8
Indonesia	28.2
Nigeria	24.8
Brazil	24.7
Algeria	23.9
Poland	22.7
Turkey	18.0
Argentina	16.6
Mexico	16.4
Thailand	15.4
Iran, Islamic Rep. of	14.0
Egypt	13.6
India	13.0
Iraq	11.2
Philippines	10.5
Hong Kong SAR	10.1
Venezuela	6.2
South Africa	6.1
Morocco	6.0

Source: Berne Union and International Monetary Fund (IMF).

The industrial country ECAs' contribution is especially great in twenty developing and transition countries (see Table 10.2). In 1996, Russia and China accounted for slightly more than 20 percent of ECAs' worldwide exposure. Indonesia, Nigeria, Brazil, Algeria, and Poland accounted for another 30 percent. Thirteen other countries accounted for 30 percent, while the rest of the world (more than 100 countries) took the remaining 20 percent of ECA exposure.

Industrial countries hosted the first private export credit insurers in the world: Federal of Switzerland (formed in 1906), Trade Indemnity of the UK (1918), and Societe Francaise d' Assurance du Credit of France (COFACE) (1927).[2] The first private domestic credit insurer also was formed in an industrial country: American Credit Indemnity (ACI) of the United States (formed in 1892). Other privately owned export credit insurers have been in active operation in Europe since the 1930s (such as

Nederlandsche Creditverzekering Maastschappij [NCM] of the Netherlands and Hermes of Germany), but they often act as agents for government, with the risks of nonpayment also being assumed by the government. The same was true in the United States from 1963 to the late 1980s when the privately owned Foreign Credit Insurance Association (FCIA) syndicate wrote export credit insurance with co-insurance and reinsurance from the government-owned export-import bank.

In the 1990s, the situation with regard to private export credit insurance changed dramatically in the industrial countries.[3] Early in the decade, Export Credits Guarantee Department (ECGD) of the United Kingdom sold its short-term export credit insurance operations to NCM. In France, a majority of COFACE's stock was sold to the private sector, and in Belgium, NAMUR and COBAC (already privately owned) expanded their operations. In the United States, American International Group (AIG) greatly increased its wholly private operations, FCIA broke off from Eximbank, and Exporters Insurance Company (EIC) also started fully private underwriting. By the mid-1990s, additional privately owned insurers were actively writing export credit insurance in North America and Europe.

Exporters Insurance Company offers a particularly interesting innovation to exporters. EIC is the first "group captive" export credit insurance company. Domiciled in Bermuda, EIC is owned by its users, called "preference shareholders." In return for a minimum investment of $100,000 in EIC stock, each preference shareholder receives entitlement to export credit insurance outstanding equal to twenty-five times its shareholding. Exporters and banks from many countries are now preference shareholders in EIC, which substantially expanded its operations from inception in 1990 to the year 2000.

By 2000, COFACE of France had emerged as the clear leader in the privatization and internationalization of export credit insurance. COFACE now has subsidiaries and partners in Europe, Africa, Asia, and North and South America. Over a third of COFACE's private market credit insurance premium is generated outside France, and the firm is widely acknowledged as a new kind of supranational insurer, reinsurer, and provider of credit information and debt collection assistance.

One of the major factors behind the increasing privatization and internationalization of export credit insurance is the growing prevalence of multinational companies as exporters and importers. These ultrasophisticated firms seek insurance of all kinds from around the world to maximize cost/benefit calculations and to minimize bureaucracy and red tape—particularly requirements for national origin, minimum cash payments, and repayment terms. By the late 1990s, it was estimated that one-third of world exports were made by multinationals to outside parties and another third were made to subsidiary companies. The mul-

11

Developing Countries

Developing countries offer the same kinds of export credit, guarantee, and insurance programs as their industrial country counterparts.[1] The developing countries usually start by offering rediscount facilities, then follow with pre-shipment guarantee programs and post-shipment export credit insurance coverage. The need for export credit, guarantee, and insurance facilities is closely related to the type of products a country exports, current and potential export markets, and the number and size of firms that export or potentially could export. The availability of needed financing and the capacity of the financial sector to provide adequate and appropriate financing also affect both the need and demand for export credit, insurance, and guarantee facilities. Government programs and regulations can either facilitate or hinder export development and influence how exporters and banks react to, and use, export credit insurance and guarantee programs to expand their export-related activities.

Developing country exporters face many difficulties in arranging export finance, which often put them at a disadvantage compared with industrial country counterparts.[2] Major problems include the following:

1. The commercial banking sector is very conservative in the extension of credit, offering shorter terms and higher interest rates than industrial-country counterparts.
2. Banks frequently offer smaller amounts of credit to individual customers and insist on greater collateralization than in industrialized countries.

3. Developing country banks are often less experienced and less well connected internationally and are therefore less willing to make export loans.

4. Banks lack correspondents in some markets and have limited lines of credit available where correspondent relationships exist.

5. Lack of reliable information about the exporters, as well as about their foreign buyers and markets, limits banks' willingness to support nontraditional exporters.

6. Weak capitalization and a high level of problem loans at many banks strongly circumscribe possibilities for new lending.

7. Balance of payments problems in some foreign markets expose exporters to political and commercial risks, which discourage them from extending post-shipment credit.

8. No trading of bankers' acceptances occurs, so banks have limited sources of funding for export transactions.

9. No pre-shipment guarantee or post-shipment insurance scheme is in place to encourage exporting and lending to exporters.

10. Banks do not focus on export credit as a functional speciality, but rather offer classical international banking services composed largely of letters of credit, international documentary collections, and foreign exchange.

11. Traditional working capital lines of credit, which coincidentally are used to finance exports, are fully collateralized with cash, securities, or property.

12. Personal guarantees and, in the case of multinational enterprises, guarantees from parent corporations may be accepted but only from larger, better-known companies.

13. Relationship banking is the rule and transnational, cash flow-based credit facilities are a rare exception granted to only the best customers.

14. Modern disbursement methods for export-related credits and the associated self-liquidating nature of trade transactions are not clearly and widely understood by individual bankers.

15. Special financial needs of exporters receive scant recognition from government and the private sector.

Different regions of the developing world have shown different trends of export credit agency (ECA) development. In Africa, for example, relatively few countries had ECAs by the year 2000. Those that had active ECAs at the close of the twentieth century were mainly in North Africa (Morocco, Tunisia, and Egypt) and Southern Africa (South Africa, Lesotho, Swaziland, Zambia, and Zimbabwe). Nigeria, Senegal, Guinea, and Ghana also had specialized ECAs, and export finance programs were located in other financial institutions in Cote d'Ivoire, Kenya, Mauritius, Tanzania, and Uganda.

In Latin America, all of the large- and medium-sized countries had ECAs—most of them of long standing—by 2000. This was true in Argentina, Brazil, Chile, Colombia, Mexico, Peru, and Venezuela. Chile's ECA was relatively new and totally private sector oriented. Recent adjustments had been made and/or new institutions existed along with the old in Brazil, Colombia, and Venezuela. None of the small Latin American countries had free-standing ECAs, although about half had export credit rediscount programs offered by central banks or other agencies. Among countries offering rediscount programs were Ecuador, Uruguay, Costa Rica, El Salvador, Guatemala, and Honduras.

In the English-speaking Caribbean, active specialized ECAs exist in Jamaica, Trinidad and Tobago, the Eastern Caribbean States, and Barbados (in the last two, the ECA is located in the central bank). In Asia, all of the large countries and high-performing East Asian economies had active ECAs by 2000.[3] The only countries without national ECAs were some of the smaller nations in Southeast Asia (Burma, Cambodia, and Laos) and some Middle Eastern countries (Iran, Iraq, and Saudi Arabia).

Developing country ECAs have generally displayed better financial results than their industrial country counterparts. Most developing ECAs have been profitable after the first few years of operation, and they have shown dynamic expansion despite the special problems posed by difficult financial environments. There are a number of reasons why developing country ECAs have shown better financial performance than industrial country ECAs:

- Better market spread
- Shorter credit terms
- A determination not to subsidize exports at the expense of financial viability
- Better planning at start-up
- Greater reliance on external technical assistance
- More willingness to learn from the mistakes of others

The better foreign market spread and shorter credit terms of developing country ECAs are because their countries' exports are largely directed to the industrial world. ECA subsidies cannot be afforded by developing countries. The other reasons noted are the result of the ECAs' decisions to maximize their professionalism.

The services provided by individual export credit agencies reflect the requirements of their exporters. In most developing countries, for example, the bulk of exports consists of agricultural products, raw materials, and consumer goods. These exports are usually sold on short-term credit with a maturity of well under a year. In such cases, insurance to the exporter, or guarantees to the exporter's bank, and short-term rediscount operations for both pre- and post-shipment will handle most of the exporters' requirements. In these countries, a good ECA will also

Table 11.1
Programs Offered by Developing Country ECAs as of December 31, 1995

PROGRAMS OFFERED BY DEVELOPING COUNTRY ECAs
As of December 31, 1995

Programs	Pre-Shipment Guarantees	Pre-Shipment Insurance	Post-Shipment Guarantees	Post-Shipment Insurance	Pre-Shipment Finance	Post-Shipment Finance	Plant & Equipment Guarantees	Plant & Equipment Finance	Foreign Exchange Insurance	Performance Guarantees
Argentina	X	X	X	X	X	X	X			
Bangladesh	X	X	X	X	X	X	X	X		
Barbados	X	X	X	X	X	X				
Brazil					X	X				
Cameroon	X	X		X	X					
China	X			X	X					
Colombia	X		X	X	X		X			
Cote d'Ivoire				X						
Czech Rep.		X		X	X	X				
Ecuador					X	X		X		
Hong Kong	X	X	X	X						
Hungary		X	X	X	X	X				
India	X	X	X	X	X	X	X	X	X	
Indonesia	X		X	X						X
Jamaica	X		X	X	X	X				
Lesotho				X	X					
Liberia			X							
Malaysia			X	X	X	X				X

76

Table 11.1 (*Continued*)

PROGRAMS OFFERED BY DEVELOPING COUNTRY ECA's
As of December 31, 1995

Programs	Pre-Shipment Guarantees	Pre-Shipment Insurance	Post-Shipment Guarantees	Post-Shipment Insurance	Pre-Shipment Finance	Post-Shipment Finance	Plant & Equipment Guarantees	Plant & Equipment Finance	Foreign Exchange Insurance	Performance Guarantees
Mauritius	X	X	X	X						
Mexico	X	X	X	X	X	X				X
Peru	X	X	X		X	X				
Philippines	X									
Poland			X	X	X	X				
Romania	X		X		X	X				
Senegal			X		X			X		
Singapore	X	X	X	X	X	X				X
Slovenia			X	X	X	X				
South Africa		X		X	X				X	
South Korea	X	X		X	X	X				X
Swaziland			X		X	X				
Taiwan		X	X	X	X	X				X
Thailand				X	X	X				
Trinidad	X		X	X	X	X				
Turkey			X	X	X	X				X
Uruguay			X	X	X					
Venezuela	X	X		X	X	X				
Zambia		X			X	X				
Zimbabwe		X	X	X	X	X				X

provide a lot of technical advice and, in some cases, credit information and country risk analysis services.

In 1995, the United Nations Conference on Trade and Development (UNCTAD) tabulated the program offerings of most developing country ECAs.[4] This demonstrated the tremendous diversity of pre- and post-shipment finance facilities available to the exporters of developing countries (see Table 11.1).

As shown, many developing country ECAs offer a full range of export credit, guarantee, and insurance programs. Those ECAs that have been in business for the longest time generally offer the widest variety of programs. There are two areas where developing country ECAs are often more active than their industrial country counterparts: pre-shipment guarantees and plant and equipment guarantees/finance. The former reflects the greater conservatism of developing country commercial banks in lending to exporters without guarantees and the latter reflects the fact that longer-term financing for exporters' own plant and equipment is very hard to obtain from private sources in many developing countries.

NOTES

1. First Washington Associates, *International Comparisons: Export Finance and Promotion Study* (Arlington, VA: FWA, 1991), chap. I.

2. United Nations Conference on Trade and Development, *Trade Financing in Developing Countries: An Assessment and Evaluation of Existing Schemes and Future Requirements* (Geneva, Switzerland: UNCTAD, 1991), chap. I.

3. Asian Development Bank, *Export Finance: Some Asian Examples* (Manila, Philippines: ADB, 1990), 7–24.

4. United Nations Conference on Trade and Development, *Review of Progress in Trade Finance Facilities of Developing Countries at the Interregional, Regional and Subregional Levels* (Geneva, Switzerland: UNCTAD, 1996), 44–71.

12

Transition Countries

The transition countries of Central and Eastern Europe and Central Asia, so-called because they are making the transition from communism to capitalism, face a number of special trade finance problems:[1]

- Strong concentration of financial resources within a few banks
- Unstable financial position of many banking institutions, which suffer from nonperforming and bad debts
- High interest rates, focus on short-term loans, and excessive collateral requirements
- Inadequate legal and institutional frameworks, including poor contract enforcement, inability to support creditor-borrower relationships and to perfect security to creditors
- Imbalances in the geographic coverage of banks
- Slow and inefficient payment systems
- Lack of access to reliable and current information on exporters, importers, and buying countries
- Lack of trade financing instruments, such as banker's acceptances, and of experience of banks and their clients in the use of documentary credit and documentary collection
- Inexperience of bank personnel in trade finance programs, policies, and procedures
- Conservative attitude of banks to risk-taking

In order to address these problems, since the beginning of the 1990s most of the Central and Eastern European countries and several Central Asian countries have established official export credit agencies (ECAs).[2] The main purpose of their operation is to assist exporters in obtaining cheaper financing either through government credits or through private bank loans supported by state guarantees.

Individual ECAs in this region differ considerably. In Poland and Latvia, for example, governments concentrate on providing export credit insurance. The latter is accepted by local banks as collateral, and this allows exporters to get preferential loan terms. In the Czech Republic and Hungary, two types of government agencies exist, dealing separately with export insurance and export financing. They operate independently but in close cooperation. Thus, in the Czech Republic, the Export Guarantee and Insurance Corporation (EGAP) insures export transactions, while long- and medium-term export financing is the responsibility of the Czech Export Bank (CEB). Loans received by the exporters from the CEB must be insured with the EGAP. In Romania, the Slovak Republic, Slovenia, and Kazakstan, there is a single state agency—an export-import bank or export corporation—that provides both direct financing and state guarantees; in certain cases, insurance against political and commercial risks is also offered. Often such public entities provide guarantees for both exports and imports.

The Newly Independent States (NIS) had no specialized export guarantee/insurance schemes until the early 1990s when several insurance programs were started with the participation of foreign capital. Thus, the Uzbek National Insurance Company (Uzbekinvest) in 1995 founded a joint venture with an American insurance company—American International Group Inc. (AIG). The new London-based company Uzbekinvest International Company is 80 percent owned by the Uzbek government with the balance of shares held by AIG. The main field of activity of this venture is insurance of foreign investors against confiscation, expropriation, and other risks, and also insurance for exporters against commercial and political risks.

In Russia, an export-import bank was established in 1993 to offer a variety of trade credit, guarantee, and insurance programs. However, as late as 1999 the organization had remained relatively inactive, due largely to government budgetary problems and competing priorities in a time of great economic turmoil. In Bosnia-Herzegovina, a new agency—Guarantee Administration Unit (FIGA)—was established in 1996 with World Bank assistance. FIGA provides political risk guarantees to foreign companies selling goods on credit to Bosnian firms for processing and subsequent export. The World Bank is also financing conversion of the Export-Import Bank of Ukraine into a full-service ECA. Georgia, Armenia, and other CIS countries were considering the establishment of ECAs in the mid-1990s but had taken no concrete actions as late as 1999.

Figure 12.1
Structure of the World Bank Pre-Export Guarantee Facility

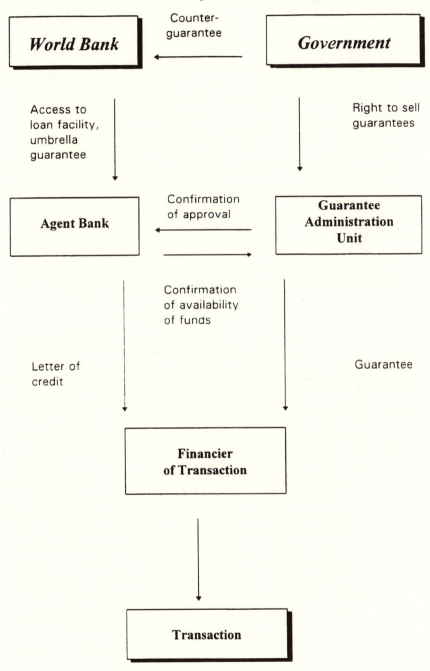

In terms of their geographical coverage, ECAs in the Central and Eastern European (CEE) countries are primarily oriented toward increasing sales to industrial countries. In Slovenia, the Organization for Economic Cooperation and Development (OECD) countries in 1995 accounted for 70 percent of total volume of political risk insurance issued. In the Czech Republic, in 1995, the bulk of commercial risks insurance concerned exports to developed market economies (82 percent of all policies). However, almost all of the political risks covered by the Czech EGAP were in China, Iran, Kazakstan, and the Philippines. A better coverage of transition economies by CEE credit insurance schemes could help expand subregional foreign trade.

In the transition economies, multilateral development banks have been experimenting with new ways of assisting ECAs, proto-ECAs, and regular commercial banks with their trade finance programs. The World Bank, for instance, approved new types of guarantees to capitalize pre-export guarantee facilities in Albania and Bosnia-Herzegovina (see Figure 12.1). The World Bank sponsored facilities cover a variety of political risks of nonpayment when trade credits are extended to these countries in connection with the sale of raw materials, intermediate goods, and parts, which are used to produce goods for subsequent export to other countries. It is expected that the guarantee administration units in Albania and Bosnia-Herzegovina will become the nuclei for full-scale ECAs.

The EBRD has also tried new techniques in the transition economies to support short-term export and import transactions, provide guarantees for payment risks on eligible local financial institutions, and support the institutional development of commercial banks and other trade finance entities. At the end of 1996, the EBRD had approved eight trade facilitation programs, with a total value of almost $300 million, for Russia, Ukraine, Uzbekistan, Estonia, Macedonia, Lithuania, Belarus, and Hungary (see Figure 12.2).

Figure 12.2
Export Transaction Under Global Trade Facilitation Program

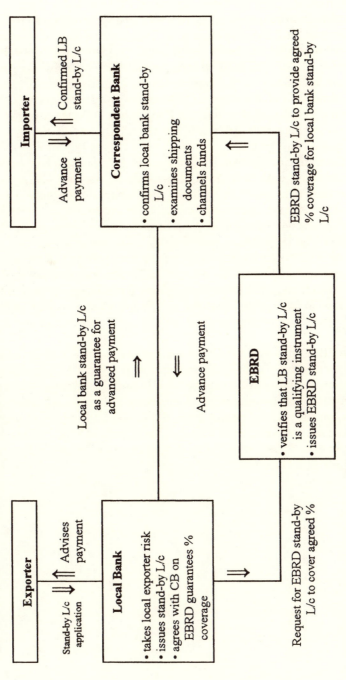

Notes: L/C = letter of credit; LB = local bank; CB = correspondent bank.

NOTES

1. Mary Watkins, ed., *World Export Credit Guide, 1998–99* (London: Euromoney Publications/Bank of America, 1998).

2. United Nations Economic Commission for Europe, *Strengthening of Export Finance Support in Central and Eastern Europe* (Geneva, Switzerland: UN/ECE-ITC, 1996), 4–5.

Regional ECAs

Regional and subregional trade financing programs are offered by multinational entities in Africa, the Middle East, the Caribbean, and Latin America (see Table 13.1). These regional organizations are capitalized largely by member countries, which share a common geographic region, culture, historical tradition, or religion.[1] The regional export credit agencies (ECAs) have many common features, but other aspects are peculiar to the individual organization. Perhaps the most outstanding common feature is their objective to provide an extra source of export finance to member countries that suffer from inadequate funds for trade finance. All the regional organizations were founded with the goal of marshaling additional funds from abroad on terms and conditions that would be better than those available to individual members. The regional ECAs give priority to nontraditional exports, and many of them are devoted mainly, and in some cases exclusively, to stimulating intraregional trade. Short-term credits are usually the main product of these organizations, although some also provide medium and even long-term facilities. Most of the regional ECAs operate as second-tier lenders, providing refinancing to commercial banks, which interface directly with exporters. Almost all of the regional organizations refuse to take the risks of nonpayment on the underlying export/import transactions. They insist that these risks be assumed by the financing banks. However, in a few cases, the regional ECAs offer export credit insurance or guarantees.

The African Export-Import Bank (AFREXIM) is one of the newest regional ECAs. It was established in 1993 as an initiative of the African

Table 13.1
Regional Trade Financing Programs

Name	Type	Inception Date	Programs	Capital
AFREXIM	Regional export credit agency	1993	Pre- & post-shipment, & direct financing	$750.0 million authorized, $145.4 million paid in (1998)
ATFP	Specialized trade finance institution	1990	Lines of Credit	$500.0 million authorized, $453.7 million paid in (1994)
BLADEX	Regional trade financial institution	1979	Refinancing of export receivables	$160.0 million authorized, $135.2 million paid in (1996)
CAF	Multilateral development bank	1970	Pre- & post-shipment, project finance, lines of credit	$2,050.0 million authorized, $821.2 million paid in (1990)
IADB	Unit of Regional development bank	1960	Pre- & post-shipment finance, lines of credit for national export credit agencies	$62,917.9 million subscribed, $3,480.8 million paid in (1995)
IAIGC	Regional export credit & investment insurance organization	1975	Export credit insurance & investment guarantees	$33.3 million authorized, $7.2 million paid in (1994)
ICIEC	Regional export credit & investment insurance agency	1995	Short & medium-term insurance, & Bank Master Policy	$89.7 million paid in (1995)
ISDB	Unit of Regional development bank	1975	Short- and long-term finance	$2,526.0 million subscribed, $2,119.6 million paid in (1989)
CABEI	Unit of Multilateral development bank	1961	Short-term finance	$50.0 million paid in (1995)
OECS	Unit of Central Bank	1984	Pre-shipment guarantees	$44.3 million (1996)
PTA Bank	Unit of Regional development bank	1985	Short-term finance, reinsurance	$74.6 million (1990)

Source: FWA, *A Summary of Regional Trade Finance Programs* (1996).

Development Bank (AFDB) and is headquartered in Cairo, Egypt. It has authorized capital of $750 million, of which $145.4 million had been paid in by early 1998. Shares are held by the AFDB, African and non-African banks, and African member governments. As of mid-1997, there were twenty-eight member countries from all parts of Africa. By the same date, AFREXIM was taking early steps in financing intra- and extra-African trade. It has authority to offer pre- and post-shipment rediscount facilities, exporter performance guarantees, direct financing including medium-term credits for essential imports for export-oriented industries, and letters of credit confirmation.

The PTA Bank, headquartered in Bujumbura, Burundi, is another African offeror of regional ECA facilities. The PTA Bank, also called the Eastern and Southern African Trade and Development Bank, was established in 1985. Most of the PTA Bank's activity is in traditional development lending, but trade finance operations were commenced in the 1990s and are expected to become a growing part of the bank's activity.

The PTA Bank has authority to offer a variety of trade finance programs to member countries of the common market for eastern and southern Africa. Among other facilities, the PTA Bank has sponsored the PTA Reinsurance Company (ZEP-Re), which aims at providing reinsurance for national ECAs in member countries.

Twenty African countries with substantial Muslim populations benefit from the regional ECA facilities of the Islamic Development Bank (IsDB). This bank was established in 1975 in Jeddah, Saudi Arabia, to aid development in forty-five Islamic countries in the Middle East, Asia, and Africa. As of 1990, the IsDB had subscribed capital of $2.5 billion, of which $2.1 billion was paid in. Most of the IsDB's activities consist of other types of development finance, but trade credit has become an important part of the bank's activity. The IsDB finances trade only between member countries, based on Islamic principles of banking. They offer rediscount facilities for medium- and long-term export credits, short-term export credits, and import credits.

Also available to Islamic countries are the facilities of the Islamic Corporation for the Insurance of Investment and Export Credit (ICIEC). Established as a subsidiary of the IsDB in 1994, the ICIEC is headquartered in Jeddah and offers export credit insurance and investment guarantees for transactions between member countries. It has paid in capital of $90 million. As of late 1999, the ICIEC had a relatively modest volume of activity but was considering ways to expand marketing and enhance utilization of its programs.

Another Middle Eastern regional ECA is the Inter Arab Investment Guarantee Corporation (IAIGC), headquartered in Kuwait City, Kuwait. The IAIGC was established in 1975 and now has twenty-one member countries. As of 1995, it had authorized capital of $53 million, of which $7 million was paid in. IAIGC offers both investment guarantees and export credit guarantees. Its operations were disrupted by the Gulf War in the early 1990s, and as late as 1997, IAIGC still had relatively low activity levels.

The Arab Trade Financing Program (ATFP) completes the list of regional ECAs in the Middle East. The ATFP was established in 1990 in Abu Dhabi, United Arab Emirates. There are shareholders from fourteen different countries. The ATFP has authorized capital of $500 million, of which $454 million was paid in by 1995. It has been active since 1991, offering lines of credit to participating banks extending from three months to three years, and exceptionally longer, to finance trade between Arab countries.

The exporters of Latin America and the Caribbean have also been major beneficiaries of regional ECA programs. The oldest and, for a long time, most active regional ECA program in the world was operated by the Inter-American Development Bank (IADB), headquartered in Washington, D.C. The IADB has paid in capital of about $4 billion and its primary activity has always been development lending. However, for a period of about twenty years, starting in the early 1970s, the IADB administered very active short- and medium-term export rediscount facilities for central banks and national ECAs in their regional member countries. The short-term facility still operates at a low level in a handful of countries.

A continuing superstar in the regional ECA field is the Latin American Bank for Exports (BLADEX), established in 1979 and headquartered in Panama City, Panama. BLADEX has mixed public-private ownership and provides short-term rediscount facilities to banks and ECAs in its twenty-two Latin American and Caribbean member countries. Profitable almost since inception, BLADEX has operated successfully at growing levels of activity for twenty years. It has set high standards of performance and has served as a model for other regional ECAs. As of early 1997, BLADEX had paid in capital of $135 million.

The Andean Development Corporation (CAF) is a traditional development bank headquartered in Caracas, Venezuela, and serving five Andean countries. Established in 1970, CAF has paid in capital of about $600 million. It administers the Andean Trade Financing System (SAFICO), offering pre- and post-shipment rediscount facilities for exporters in member countries. Related credits can be short term, medium term and, in exceptional cases, long term.

The Bank for Central American Economic Integration (CABEI), was established in Tegucigalpa, Honduras, in 1961. CABEI is primarily a development bank for its four Central American member countries. It experienced severe financial problems in the 1980s and instituted trade finance facilities only in the 1990s, concentrating on short-term rediscounting of trade paper. Activity to date has been modest. CABEI has authorized capital of almost $160 million, of which less than $30 million was paid in as of 1996.

The Organization of Eastern Caribbean States (OECS) operates a regional ECA for the states and territories of the Windward and Leeward Islands and the British Virgin Islands in the Caribbean. This facility, headquartered in the Central Bank in Basseterre, St. Kitts, issues and administers a program of pre-shipment guarantees for eligible exporters in member countries. The guarantee program was established in 1988 and has been moderately utilized since then.

Serious discussions have been held for a number of years on the possibility of establishing regional ECAs for Southern Africa, Asia, Central and Eastern Europe and Central Asia. As of 2000, none of these proposals was close to final action.

NOTE

1. First Washington Associates, *A Summary of Regional Trade Finance Programs* (Arlington, VA: FWA, 1996).

Setting Up ECAs

A number of issues arise in the course of considering whether or not a government should establish an export credit agency (ECA) and how that ECA should be organized and managed to achieve the objectives sought. The first question to be answered is how these facilities would benefit the country, its exporters, bankers, and other interested parties. Good reasons for the establishment of ECAs are (1) to increase exports in order to redress balance of payments problems; (2) to promote domestic economic development through increased production, which creates employment and contributes to capital investment and/or more efficient utilization of domestic productive capacity; and (3) to help small- and medium-sized firms that lack access to the capital markets.[1]

To achieve an increase in exports, official ECA programs are designed to reduce exporters' risks and increase their access to bank financing. This in turn allows exporters to extend credit to foreign buyers on terms that are more competitive with those offered by their counterparts in other countries. If these facilities encourage additions to a country's exports, the balance of payments of the country will improve, assuming that imports do not increase at a faster rate. Obviously, an increase in production for export will result in expansion of employment and utilization of productive capacity.

Export credit programs are meant to supplement the activities of commercial banks by assuming risks and extending credit where banks are unable or unwilling to participate. Also, the programs can be an inducement to commercial banks to finance exports where they would not do so otherwise and thus contribute to the development of the commercial banking system as a whole. Official export finance programs usually result in improved availability of credit information on countries and foreign buyers; this is useful to both exporters and the commercial banking system. The expansion of export activity in itself familiarizes both bankers and exporters with various dimensions of risk and methods of reducing that risk, which is beneficial for general business and economic development. Small- and medium-size firms are often the greatest beneficiaries of ECA programs because they have been the most deprived of the finance and skills necessary for international success.

In addition to the benefits, one must consider the actual and potential costs of export credit, guarantee, and insurance facilities. The assumption of risks can mean potentially large losses to the ECAs, exporters, and commercial banks due to the inability of buyers to pay for exports in a timely manner. Extension of credit for sales to foreign buyers can result in less credit being available for domestic needs. If credit is extended on below market terms, a subsidy is created, which has a cost that must be absorbed. Furthermore, ECA programs entail an administrative cost, both to set up and to operate. Poor reasons to establish an official ECA include the following:

1. *Encouraging exports to poor payors.* Exports that are not paid for are not really helpful to exporters, banks, or the exporting country. They have no beneficial impact on the balance of payments and have an adverse impact on the exporting government's finances.

2. *Subsidizing the costs of credit.* This may provide some cosmetic benefits to exports in the short term, but in the long run, it will either bankrupt the ECA or erode public support for its operations because of the cost to the taxpayer.

3. *Substituting for an aid program.* Attempts to substitute an ECA for an aid program are unwise, inasmuch as the ECA's sponsors will expect it to operate in a sound, businesslike fashion, which cannot be done if its main goal becomes the extension of development finance to poor countries.

4. *Undercutting credit terms.* Continual extension of export credit terms beyond generally accepted norms is increasingly expensive and ultimately defeating to the ECA. Also, longer and longer export credits have greater risks of nonpayment and are not necessarily beneficial to the exporting country's balance of payments.

5. *Propping up inefficient domestic industries.* These firms generally have bad credit characteristics and do not represent the future of a country's exports. Association of an ECA with fundamentally flawed exporters can impair its own finances and limit its ability to assist other exporters that are dynamic and economically sound.

Thus, in deciding whether or not to initiate export credit, guarantee, and insurance programs, the developing country must weigh the potential benefits against the potential costs. It is not clear that all countries need these programs, nor are all programs necessarily useful for any one country. Clearly, the choice of programs that will yield desired results is critical. Programs must be tailored to meet the specific requirements of the country. Determination of acceptable costs versus potential benefits is a policy decision that the government must make. The private sector can assume some of these functions without government sanction if the potential for profit is sufficient, but it may not be willing to assume enough risks to meet all the programs' needs. Particularly in the area of foreign political risks, private banks and insurance companies in most countries have preferred not to take those risks, and it has been necessary for government to assume the political risks in order to permit ECAs to offer full coverage to exporters.

In order to determine whether export credit, guarantee and insurance programs are justified, the potential sponsors of ECAs should consider a number of factors, including the composition and characteristics of current and potential exports, as well as the capacity of existing financial institutions to meet expected growth. It should first be determined if the country has sufficient actual or potential volume of exports to establish cost-effective programs. Usually the country must have at least $100 million of manufactured exports in order to justify the establishment of official credit facilities and meet all the attendant administrative costs of operations.[2] Countries that have little potential to expand the volume and variety of export production have little need for export credit, guarantee, and insurance programs. Countries whose products are not quality- and price-competitive should not establish such facilities, nor should those which are unprepared to initiate the marketing effort necessary to produce substantial export orders. Another question to be answered is whether there are sufficient numbers of actual and potential exporters to justify the programs contemplated. The expense may not be justified or politically acceptable if the ECA serves the needs of a small number of exporters or serves the needs of only large, well-established exporters.

The demand for an ECA's trade finance products is strongly affected by the following:

- the extent of traditional vs. nontraditional exports (the former being chiefly commodities that are purchased for cash and traded in international commodities exchanges, and the latter being more often the subject of financing between buyer and seller)
- the types of nontraditional exports involved (certain products by their nature require longer or shorter periods of payment and different documentary terms)
- the extent of sales between affiliated companies versus sales between nonaffiliated firms (the former usually being done on open account without bank

involvement and the latter usually involving bank credit and/or letters of credit or other documentary terms)

- whether the exports are going to industrial or developing countries (the former being perceived as less risky with correspondingly less bank involvement and the latter being perceived as more risky with greater use of bank letters of credit and documentary collections)

- whether exports are within or outside a fully functioning customs and political union (if they are within the European Union [EU] or North American Free Trade Association [NAFTA], for example, exports are increasingly regarded and treated like domestic sales with a corresponding drop in use of international trade finance products)

- the size of buyers (smaller firms in general finding it more difficult to arrange credit)

- the size of exporters (smaller firms in general finding a need to arrange more secure means of payment, but having less leverage to demand such terms)

Assuming sufficient volume, good quality, and competitive price of goods, the exporters' position with regard to credit needs to be assessed. For example, what are the normal credit terms for their products in international trade and what do competitors offer? Are sales being lost because of credit terms? Do exporters have to extend longer than normal credit terms because their products are less well known in the market?

A basic question concerning risk assumption is where do exporters sell their products? Do these markets pose high risks with regard to availability of foreign exchange and political stability or are they relatively stable? Are the foreign buyers in industries that are stable, growing, or declining? Are exporters aware of potential market opportunities and hesitant to pursue them because of perceived commercial or political risks? Are banks hesitant to finance exporters in some markets because of political or commercial risks? Answers to all of these questions can be ascertained through interviews with exporters and bankers and through various trade organizations.

A further consideration in deciding whether to establish export credit, guarantee, and insurance programs is the capacity of existing financial institutions and governments to allocate resources to such programs and the availability of personnel to administer the programs, either in government or in the private sector. The types of programs and the administering entity are two major issues that must be considered in deciding how to implement export credit, guarantee, and insurance facilities.

PROGRAM OFFERINGS

In analyzing the needs for different types of programs, ECAs should know the percentage of goods that require financing in their countries and the appropriate terms of payment. Such terms of payment are usually quite short: less than 180 days.[3] The Export-Import Bank of the United States (U.S. Eximbank) made a comprehensive investigation of national credit-term requirements twenty years ago but has not repeated the exercise more recently. Its main findings were that two-thirds of U.S. exports were not financed at all; they were paid in cash or within thirty days of shipment based upon credit extended solely by the exporter. Of the one-third of national exports that received some financing, most financing came from commercial banks without any ECA backing. The ECA's financing amounted to less than 10 percent of total national exports. The same study found that the average repayment term of U.S. export finance for sales to all regions of the world was very short. Financing under one year accounted for 80 to 90 percent of all financing extended on sales to Organization for Economic Cooperation and Development (OECD) countries and over 50 percent of all financing extended to developing countries. Financing with a term over five years accounted for less than 15 percent of all financing.

The U.S. Eximbank also confirmed that the terms of financing were heavily dependent upon the types of products being sold. Ninety percent of basic commodities exports from the United States, if they received financing at all, were paid for in less than one year. Eighty-seven percent of manufactured noncapital goods financing had a term of less than one year, and 60 percent of most capital equipment financing was paid in less than one year. In contrast, only 17 percent of heavy transportation equipment financing was repaid in less than one year. The latter group was the only one in which *most* goods were financed and *most* financing had a term over five years.

With respect to post-shipment financing, the following questions need to be answered: (1) Is adequate financing available to exporters from existing sources to enable them to extend competitive credit terms to foreign buyers or is supplemental financing required? (2) If adequate financing is not available, can actions be taken other than direct lending by government to exporters or through commercial banks that would make the necessary financing available? (3) Does government or the private sector have sufficient resources that they are willing to direct to such a program? (4) Is below market rate financing necessary for exporters to be competitive and if so, how will resources be obtained to provide funds at low rates?

In establishing an export credit financing facility, it is important to consider the effects on commercial banks, whose co-operation and support are essential. It is unlikely that any government has sufficient resources to assume the entire export financing task, nor is it desirable for it to do so. Thus, export financing facilities should be viewed in all cases as supplementing or facilitating bank financing rather than replacing it.

On the other hand, in establishing an export credit insurance facility, it is necessary that it be perceived as financially sound, permanent, able to insure risky transactions as well as relatively safe ones, and capable of paying all claims promptly. To do this, the organization must have sufficient resources, capable staff, competent administration, and a psychology of risk-taking rather than risk-avoidance.

Two other important policy issues to consider are what risks to cover and what types of coverage to offer. The analysis of exports—in particular the markets served and the length of terms required—and the needs of exporters and banks provides information on what risks could usefully be covered to encourage expansion of exports. Sales to government entities and private buyers in countries experiencing economic and political problems may require political risk insurance coverage or both political and commercial coverage, while sales to more stable countries may require only commercial credit insurance.

In most countries, short-term coverage is sufficient to meet the majority of export credit insurance requirements. However, as countries industrialize and export more manufactured goods, longer term coverage is increasingly needed. Sales of capital equipment and other goods often require medium-term credit of one to five years, for which insurance is required due to additional uncertainty about future political and commercial risk. Exports of services, goods on consignment, and other types of exports suggest other possible coverage requirements. The initial choice of which insurance policies to offer should reflect the current and expected needs for some time. Virtually all existing export credit insurance programs have started with short-term coverage and gradually expanded coverage as needs developed.

After determining what export credit, guarantee and insurance programs would be useful, a key consideration is how the programs should best be implemented. The two major issues to be considered are the appropriate institutional risk-sharing and the most effective organizational structure.

INSTITUTIONAL RISK-SHARING

Government and government agencies, private and public sector commercial banks, and insurance companies can participate in risk assumption in guarantee and insurance programs. What the appropriate risk assumption is in any country depends on the type of programs offered and the capacity, resources, and willingness of each possible participant to be involved. In all countries with successful export credit, guarantee, and insurance schemes, the government plays an important role and, in many instances, is the sole provider of these programs and assumes all risks.

Political risk export credit insurance coverage has produced greater losses on sales to developing country markets than commercial risk coverage. However, these losses are usually recoverable to a greater degree, after a long waiting period, than commercial risk losses. Because of the magnitude of potential losses, political risk coverage is typically assumed by government. Private banks and insurance companies assumed significant and growing political risks in the 1990s, and it is assumed they will continue to do so in the future. However, private companies have less ability to deal with governments of other countries to resolve payment problems. Because they operate with profit objectives, private sector companies theoretically are less likely to assume the full range of political risks and may charge higher premiums to underwrite selected political risks than governments whose primary interest is expanding national exports.

Commercial risk, which is based on specific transactions to particular buyers, lends itself more to underwriting by private sector entities or consortia. Claims and losses are likely to be smaller, both individually and collectively. The private sector may have a better capacity to evaluate commercial risks and, in some instances, be willing to assume more risk than government. Administration may be more streamlined and responsive to exporters than government programs.

The drawbacks to private sector participation in commercial risk insurance are that companies may not have the capacity to underwrite a sufficient volume of insurance to meet a wide variety of exporter's needs; they may choose to insure only the better risks or charge higher premiums for riskier buyers; and they may be also less likely to deal with smaller and less established exporters who may encounter problems due to inexperience.

Where government and private companies both offer commercial risk insurance, private companies may insure the best risks, leaving the more risky situations for government insurance. As a result, the government programs may not be willing to assume the same amount of risk as they would if they had a greater spread of risk between less and more risky transactions or the programs may not be able to operate without heavy losses over time due to concentration of poorer risks. For reasons such as these, only large countries can usually support more than one export credit insurer.

It is clear that government usually must play a significant role in assumption of political risk. Private companies may take some or all of the commercial risks. Risk sharing can be structured in many ways. For example, private companies can assume risks up to a certain amount for a country or a buyer, with the government taking the remaining risks. Alternatively, risks can be shared on each transaction on a fixed percentage basis, or private companies can take all risks on the early maturities of medium- and long-term business, with government taking all risks on the later maturities. Another approach is to obtain private reinsurance inside or outside the country, which can limit the amount of resources government or domestic private companies need to devote to the facilities.

APPROPRIATE ORGANIZATIONAL STRUCTURE

Several choices exist as to how the export credit, guarantee, and insurance facilities can be organized. The key policy questions are who should have ownership, who should manage the facility, and should the facility be autonomous or tied to some other entity.

Logically, ownership should reflect the risk sharing and relative contribution of resources. The arguments for government ownership are that the government has more resources and has a greater interest in promoting exports than the private sector. Also, since government is likely to assume the greatest share of risk, particularly political risk, it should have the sole or majority ownership position. Arguments for private sector ownership include removing the ECA from politics, stabilizing its finances, and increasing the chances that it will be responsive to exporters and run in a businesslike fashion. If some private sector ownership is sought, it appears essential that ownership be broad based to gain the advantage of many companies' resources. Private sector ownership of the facility should not favor or hinder shareholders versus nonshareholders in use of the ECA's programs. Broad-based private sector ownership may also increase exporter confidence in the ECA.

Establishment of an autonomous new institution to manage export credit, guarantee, and insurance programs has the advantage of separating these programs from other government and private sector activities, which may affect the ECA's operation and the staff and budget resources available for administration. Creation of an autonomous entity should also reduce the possibility that political pressures will compromise commercial objectives. The major disadvantage of creating a new, separate organization is the administrative cost, which is likely to exceed what would be required if programs were established in an existing organization.

Another option is to use private sector management of an autonomous organization, whether government owned or jointly owned. In effect, the private sector organization would act as an agent providing expertise; thus, the advantages of autonomous organization would be maintained. Government may be hesitant to adopt an approach where it relinquishes control. However, policy decisions with respect to the type of coverage as well as large commitments or commitments to certain countries could remain with government, and the more typical transactions could be decided by the management of the organization. Whatever decision is made with respect to management, the most important requirement is that it be efficient and able to respond quickly to exporters' needs. Inefficient management will forfeit exporters' confidence; consequently, the programs will not be used extensively. Autonomous, high-quality management seems to be a key factor in the success of export credit, guarantee, and insurance schemes.

OTHER FACTORS DETERMINING EFFECTIVENESS

Two other practical issues must be addressed by ECAs, both of which are critically important to the success of such programs. One issue is the need for any program to balance risk and cost. To be effective in encouraging exports, ECA programs must meet exporters' needs. This means assuming risks that may result in significant losses. Export credit insurance and guarantees should be viewed from an insurance perspective rather than solely a banking one. Insurance underwriting assumes that over a period of time an overall profit will be realized but that at various times losses will be incurred. Programs that do not experience any losses are rarely effective because it usually means that they are totally risk averse and thus not performing the service for which they were established. Excessive risk taking, on the other hand, can result in costs in the long term exceeding revenues, which weakens and may ultimately destroy the viability of the ECA. If that happens, the ECA can be of no further assistance to the export community.

A second issue is the impact of political pressure on the policies and procedures of export credit, guarantee, and insurance programs. Political concerns can have both positive and negative effects. On the positive side, the administrators of the ECA can be induced to take a more promotional attitude toward approving transactions. Special relationships between countries can be developed through political ties, which in turn produce improved export prospects and facilitate resolution of political risk claims for nonpayment. Because of political ties, the insurance and guarantee facilities of one country may be more willing to support exports to a particular market. In fact, some countries have special arrangements to cover exports that are perceived to be in the "national interest." In these instances, the risks of financing and insurance or guarantees are undertaken 100 percent by government because private companies rarely have equivalent political ties and therefore will not assume such risks.

Another aspect of the political environment is the potential for other government concerns and priorities to interfere with the operation of export credit, guarantee, and insurance facilities. The ECA may be pressed to underwrite unsound transactions that result in an inordinate amount of claims or loan defaults. Then, when claims have to be paid or loans rescheduled or written off, the government may be unwilling to appropriate necessary additional funds or may insist upon policy changes at the ECA that cripple its ability to be effective in the future. Government pressure for an ECA to support one economic sector rather than others can also undermine its effectiveness. Bureaucratic inefficiency, including red tape and unqualified government personnel, can make any ECA unattractive.

In summary, the ultimate success of an ECA is heavily dependent upon the thoroughness of initial efforts to firmly establish the needs for the organization and the validity of its objectives, the responsivenss of the nation's export and financial sectors, the appropriateness of its program offerings, the soundness of its initial organization, management and risk-sharing principles, and the extent to which government contributes to the ECA's objective of good financial management. Export credit agencies that start well usually end well, whereas those few that do not meet most of the above criteria have wound up doing an ineffective job of export support, often losing large sums of money in the process.

NOTES

1. Many of these observations about good and bad reasons for establishing an ECA were contributed by Malcolm Stephens, former CEO of ECGD of the United Kingdom and Secretary General of the Berne Union.

2. First Washington Associates, *A Study of Institution Building for Post-Shipment Financing, Export Credit Insurance, and Guarantees to Banks in Developing Countries* (Arlington, VA: FWA, 1986), 21.

3. Global Business Communications, *Export Credit Reports* (Gillette, NJ: GBC, 1997).

15

Legal Context

The legal context within which export credit agencies (ECAs) operate is similar in many respects to that affecting banking and insurance operations. However, because of their official character, national interest features, transnational considerations, and the special nature of many of their programs, which are really quite different from traditional banking or insurance operations, ECAs are subject to many distinctive legal considerations. Because of the unique nature of their operations, almost all ECAs work within the context of special legislation that defines their rights and responsibilities, obligations, and possibilities. This ECA legislation may be categorized as either (1) general and permissive in nature, authorizing the establishment of a company under current banking, insurance, and corporate statutes, or (2) specific in nature, establishing in detail the form, structure, powers, organization, programs, and limitations of the new export credit agency.

If the legislation is general and permissive, it is often very short, stating that it supersedes certain other legislation, that a new corporation is established to offer export credits, guarantees, or insurance under existing specified corporate or insurance laws or regulations, setting forth the minimum requirements for such operations (i.e., levels of capital and reserves in relation to outstanding insurance, minimum capital, reinsurance requirements, etc.), and the nature of interface of the new corporation with the government.

If the legislation is specific, it is usually much longer and more detailed. At a minimum, specific legislation normally contains the following:

- Statement that it supersedes previous legislation
- Name of new company
- Purpose (to offer export credits, guarantees, insurance, coinsurance, reinsurance, and related services)
- Objectives (to expand exports, to encourage domestic production and employment, etc.)
- Guiding principles (autonomy, to run organization in businesslike fashion, to be responsive to the needs of the private sector, to seek reasonable assurance of repayment, to meet foreign competition, etc.)
- Programs (types of exporter credits, guarantees, insurance, technical assistance, advisory services, etc.)
- Equity (total amounts to be authorized and paid in, types of shares and shareholders, etc.)
- Guardian authority (or regulatory authority)
- Board of directors (composition, how selected, tenure)
- Organization (principal officer(s), how selected)
- Reserves (amount, utilization, principles of managing)
- Maximum relationship between capital and reserves and outstanding exposure (gearing)
- Decision-making apparatus (credit committee, board of directors, government)
- Reinsurance by government (types of risks covered, precedence of utilization, etc.)
- Reinsurance by foreign and national reinsurance companies (general statement)
- National interest operations (to act as agent for government in certain operations, principles for sharing risks and rewards, agency(s) with which it coordinates, etc.)
- Tax status (tax-exemption for most ECAs)
- Authority to conduct operations in foreign exchange (to borrow and lend, to hold accounts overseas and transact with foreign entities)

In North America, the legislation establishing ECAs has been very specific, with the powers, duties, responsibilities, and restrictions spelled out in great detail. In the case of the Export-Import Bank of the United States (U.S. Eximbank),[1] its legislation is of a so-called sunset nature, meaning that the bank is authorized to make new commitments only during a relatively short, multi-year period, at the end of which the institution expires (i.e., its sun sets) unless renewal legislation is approved by the U.S. Congress. Also, the U.S. Eximbank's legislation is full of special restrictions and directives reflecting the fact that it has been reviewed by Congress dozens of times since original enactment in 1934.

In the English-speaking Caribbean, some semi-autonomous ECAs were created by a "memorandum and articles of association," along British lines, which covered them under a Companies Act and endowed them with a wide variety of powers, many of which were excessive to the strict needs of an official ECA. In South America, some ECAs are parts of central banks, and they have no special legislation. Other ECAs are divisions of development banks and operate under the specialized bank's legislation. Also, in the larger countries, there are semi-autonomous free-standing ECAs that have their own legislation granting specific powers and usually excluding them from the normal regulatory system.

In other countries, ECA legislation is also crafted to conform with the prevailing general system of law. Thus, for example, in the Middle East and North Africa, several of the ECAs are required to conform with the requirements of Islamic law, or Shariah. In the former Soviet Union, ECAs are still influenced by the requirements formerly imposed by socialist law. Sub-Saharan African ECAs are governed by local legal requirements as well as the commercial codes introduced by former colonial powers. Asian ECAs have their own special legal requirements and the Chinese Export-Import Bank and Peoples Insurance Corporation are fully subject to the peculiar requirements of the Chinese Communist legal system.

NOTE

1. United States Eximbank, *Laws Relating to the Export-Import Bank of the United States* (Washington, DC: U.S. Eximbank, 1993), 43.

16

Capitalization and Reinsurance

To establish export credit, guarantee, and insurance agencies, substantial capitalization is required to design and set up the organization; develop programs, systems and procedures; and hire and train qualified personnel. Initial capitalization must be sufficient to provide reserves against losses with a comfortable margin for the unexpected. In addition, it must be large enough to cover operating expense requirements during the start-up period. The amount and sources of capital are among the first issues that must be resolved by an export credit agency (ECA), since its initial capitalization will have an overwhelming effect upon its subsequent success or failure.

Because of development and start-up expenses, very few ECAs have been able to show operational profits during the first year or so after start-up. Initial capitalization is invested in interest-bearing securities in order to earn revenues that offset operational losses. As premium income builds over time, these operational losses can be converted into profits. How fast this occurs depends mainly on how rapidly the volume of insured exports increases and the level of claims. In light of these factors, newer ECAs in developing countries frequently have more rigorous capitalization standards than the older, well-established ECAs in industralial nations.[1]

The capital contribution by government and/or private entities should be fully paid in at the beginning of operations so as to be available to meet administrative expenses, pay claims, and be invested. In some countries, capital has been pledged but not paid in. This is not an optimal

Table 16.1
Capital Standards of Selected Export Finance ECAs, 1997–1998

Capital/Liabilities		Capital/Liabilities	
Australia EFIC	.06	Korea KEXIMBANK	.06
Canada EDC	.12	Norway EKSPORTFINANS	.03
Colombia BANCOLDEX	.73	Romania EXIMBANK	.37
Hungary EXIMBANK	.13	Sweden SEK	.03
India EXIMBANK	.31	Taiwan EXIMBANK	.15
Jamaica JEXIMBANK	.45		
Japan EXIMBANK	.16	Average, all 12 countries	.21

Source: Annual Reports.

situation. When funds are needed for claims, government or private companies may be reluctant or unable to contribute. Furthermore, the prospect of having to require additional funds from shareholders may cause program managers to be reluctant to take risks and thus not effectively serve exporter needs. Banks and exporters may also not have confidence in programs that are not fully funded. If government has been slow to pay in other areas, it will be assumed to be equally slow in paying money for an unfunded capital commitment.

The size of an ECA's start-up capital is usually determined by calculating the probable volume of exports to be financed in the first five or so years, estimating the related outstandings, and then projecting capital needs as a percentage of outstandings. It is usually desirable to have capital equal to at least 25 percent of outstanding actual and contingent liabilities during the first few years of ECA operation, after which greater leveraging can be acheived.

The actual positions of a number of export-important banks (eximbanks) and other export finance ECAs that are well established and operating effectively show wide differences in "leverage" or "gearing" of their capital. A study of thirteen countries showed ECA capital averaging 21 percent of actual and contingent liabilities, with a low of 3 percent and a high of 73 percent (see Table 16.1).

NEED FOR REINSURANCE

In addition to their own capital, ECAs require reinsurance or guarantees to reassure policyholders that the ECA will be able to meet all possible contingencies. Reinsurance has often been described as "supplemental" or "dedicated" capital because, like ordinary capital, it provides protection against the need for an ECA to defer payment to creditors or call on shareholders for additional funds in the event of catastrophic losses. The advantage offered by reinsurance is that it reduces the overall exposure of the export credit insurer, thereby allowing the insurer to cover a larger number of export transactions. This feature is particularly attractive to those entities with a limited paid-in capital base, which without reinsurance may be unable to meet all needs for cover.

Reinsurance is provided via treaties in which both parties agree to the terms and conditions under which export credit insurance will be offered. Treaty conditions often govern overall credit limits provided to any one buyer, the country of the buyer, percentage of cover per transaction, the proportion and method of risk-sharing between the credit insurer and the reinsurer, and the splitting of premium between the two parties.

SOURCES OF REINSURANCE

The private sector reinsurance market comprises a large number of participants, some specialists, professional reinsurers, and others for whom reinsurance is an important or occasional sideline. Professional reinsurers include three giants: Munich Reinsurance, Swiss Reinsurance, and Zurich Reinsurance, each of which has a department for credit risk evaluation. There are a number of smaller reinsurance companies in Europe and North America, many of which participate in credit treaties. In addition, many composite and other insurance companies possess reinsurance arms or sometimes participate in reinsurance treaties, not necessarily only in their core business sectors. Participation may take the form of minor shares in treaties, following the lead of companies that are recognized leaders in particular areas. Arranging reinsurance is usually difficult for newly established ECAs. However, there are reinsurance brokers and consultants who advise on this and can approach reinsurers on behalf of the ECAs.

Private-sector credit insurers often participate in one another's reinsurance treaties. A few major export credit insurers have developed the practice of partnership agreements with newly established institutions in other countries to provide help with underwriting, claims examination, recovery work, and staff training during the early period of establishing a new scheme. Such agreements may provide the new ECA with access to the international reinsurance market on more favorable terms than would otherwise be available.

REINSURANCE CONCEPTS AND GROUND RULES

The basic principles of private sector reinsurance for export credit risks are the same as for other types of reinsurance.[2] A reinsurer commits itself to bear a share of risk in return for a share of premium. If a reinsurance agreement covers a range of business, it is called a treaty. If it covers a single piece of business (comparable to a specific primary policy), it is called a facultative placement. The detailed format of reinsurance agreements varies according to the law and practice of different countries and companies.

Private sector reinsurance is normally expressed as either proportional (quota share) or nonproportional (excess of loss). Proportional reinsurance allows the primary insurer to increase the amount of business accepted through a prorata sharing of exposures. Nonproportional reinsurance allows the primary insurer to undertake payment of all losses up to an agreed amount. The balance of any loss that exceeds the agreed limit will be paid by the reinsurer up to a contractual maximum.

Quota share reinsurance has been most often used by the credit insurance market. This enables small ECAs effectively to replace paid-in capital and enables them to increase substantially the capacity that they offer. However, reinsurance programs are often a combination of quota share and excess of loss. An important clause usually found in quota share treaties provides for the reinsurer to "follow the fortunes" of the primary insurer. This means that the reinsurer is bound by decisions on underwriting and claims taken by the primary insurer. As a condition of such coverage, the primary insurer is usually required to satisfy certain decision making criteria agreed with the reinsurer.

Governments of most countries provide backing for the liabilities of their ECAs, either by reinsurance modeled on private-sector practice or—what amounts to the same thing in substance—provision by guarantee or otherwise for meeting any underwriting deficit from state funds. A reinsurance agreement between a national government and its ECA typically contains the following:

1. Names of the contracting parties (Ministry of Finance and export credit insurance company)

2. Date of commencement and term of agreement (at least five years)

3. Possibility of amendment by mutual agreement

4. Types of risks covered (first dollar for political risks-primary insurer, after exhaustion of net worth and reserves for commercial risks-reinsurer)

5. What happens if commercial risk reinsurance is obtained from other parties

6. Premium sharing (for political only, commercial only, and combined commercial/political policies.)

7. Working-capital fund for small political risk claims

8. Decision-making Apparatus (within the agreement and within ECA)

9. Levels of decision-making authority (credit committee, board of directors)

10. Principles for establishing country limits

11. Claims payment procedures (rights and obligations of both parties)

12. Recovery procedures (rights and obligations of both parties)

13. Reserving procedures by credit insurance company (e.g. when case reserves are established and removed, how much is reserved)

14. Use of reserve money, initial capital, and retained earnings to pay claims (order of precedence)

15. Dividend restrictions (on earnings from investment of initial capital and reserves)

16. Accounting principles

17. Premium-setting principles (to be set by board of directors, to encourage maximum use of program, to obtain reasonable spread or risk, to at least break even on operational basis)

18. Underwriting principles (to streamline procedures, grant discretionary or delegated authority to policyholders to maximum extent consistent with their risk-sharing and initial capabilities, and to seek reasonable assurance of repayment on all operations)

NOTES

1. Export-Import Bank of India, *Export Credit Agencies Around the World: A Comparative Analysis* (Bombay, India: Eximbank of India, 1994), 3.

2. United Nations Economic Commission for Europe, *Strengthening of Export Finance Support in Central and Eastern Europe* (Geneva, Switzerland: UN/ECE-ITC 1996), 3 of item 3d.

17

Organization and Administration

The organizational structure of export credit agencies (ECAs) differs widely, depending upon the programs that they offer, the extent to which the ECA is autonomous and free standing, the volume of its operations, the need for branch offices, the philosophy and concerns of its management, and the extent to which operations are delegated to banks and exporters.[1]

A typical organizational structure for a small, full-service ECA reflects just three main departments headed by directors and seven divisions thereunder headed by managers. Figure 17.1 depicts the export-import bank (eximbank) of a small Caribbean country, which had a total of only about three dozen employees. The organization of a large, full-service ECA in an industrial country shows certain similarities, but also many differences reflecting additional programs, operational complexities, branch offices, and a staff of about 400 (see Figure 17.2).

Each of the ECAs depicted in the organization charts is governed by a board of directors, which has general oversight and policy-making authority over the organization. However, many publicly owned ECAs—particularly in Western Europe—have a "guardian authority" in the form of a government ministry that ensures directorial responsibilities in lieu of a board. ECAs frequently also have advisory boards that give advice and guidance of a nonbinding nature. The duties of the board of directors or guardian authority generally include appointing the chief executive officer and other members of senior management; agreeing upon the basic policies and procedures to be followed by the manage-

Figure 17.1
Organization of a Small ECA

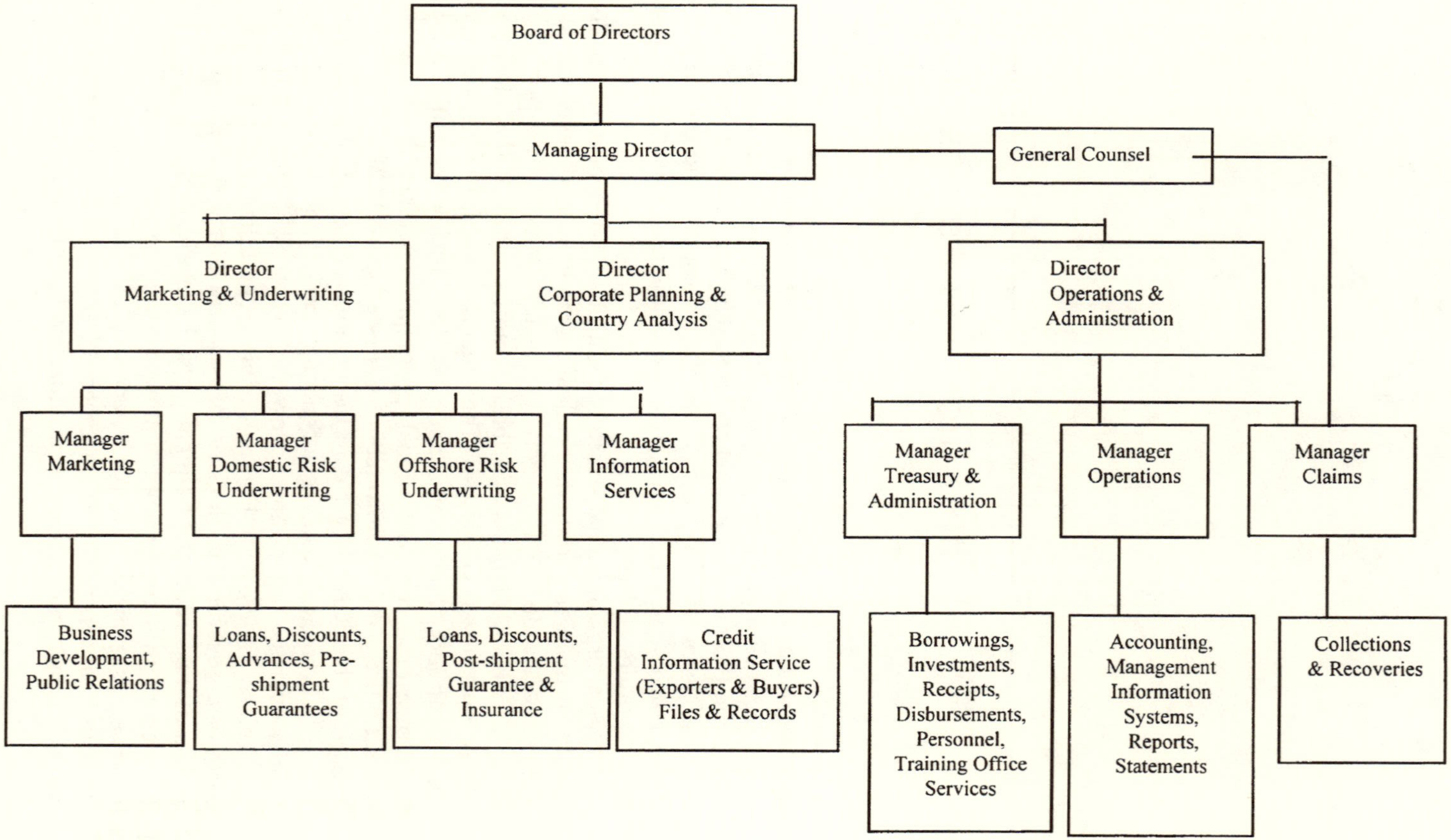

Board of Directors

Managing Director

General Counsel

Director Corporate Planning & Country Analysis

Director Operations & Administration

Director Marketing & Underwriting

Manager Claims
Collections & Recoveries

Manager Operations
Accounting, Management Information Systems, Reports, Statements

Manager Treasury & Administration
Borrowings, Investments, Receipts, Disbursements, Personnel, Training Office Services

Manager Information Services
Credit Information Service (Exporters & Buyers) Files & Records

Manager Offshore Risk Underwriting
Loans, Discounts, Post-shipment Guarantee & Insurance

Manager Domestic Risk Underwriting
Loans, Discounts, Advances, Pre-shipment Guarantees

Manager Marketing
Business Development, Public Relations

110

Figure 17.2
Organization of a Large ECA

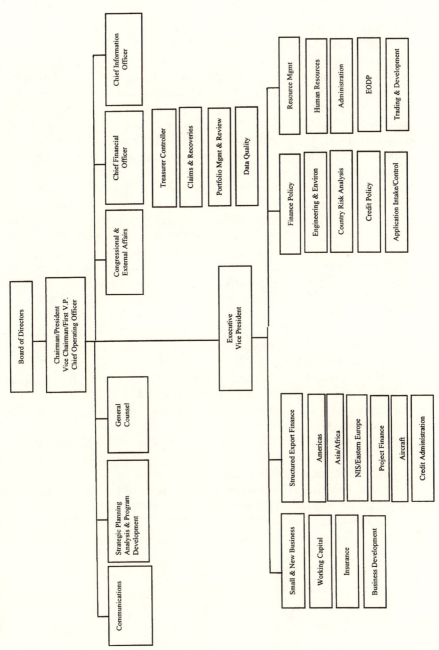

ment; approving annual budgets and reviewing performance; reviewing and approving the annual report of the organization; reviewing management's commitments of loans, guarantees, insurance and claims; and approving larger individual transactions. Usually the board has five to ten members who meet monthly or even quarterly. Sometimes, however, the board is smaller, works full time, meets weekly or even bi-weekly, and is responsible for approving all, or most, of the ECA's transactions.

Regardless of whether ownership is completely public or mixed, political risk coverage of most ECAs is assumed by the government, so decisions on country limits, large transactions, and sometimes small cases in difficult markets are often taken by a government committee. Among the entities that may be represented on such a committee are the ministries of finance or treasury, commerce or foreign trade, foreign affairs or foreign economic relations, industry or agriculture, as well as the central bank. Such committees operate separately from the ECA organization and thus are not reflected on the ECA's own organization chart.

The chief executive officer (CEO) of the ECA is usually called the president (in North and South America) or the managing director or general manager (in Europe, Africa, and elsewhere). The CEO usually has a deputy or special assistant, and the other members of senior management report to the CEO. These are the chief operating officer (COO), who is responsible for new commitments and administrative matters; the chief financial officer (CFO) who handles accounting, bookkeeping, and funds management; and the general counsel (GC) who is responsible for all legal matters affecting the ECA. Marketing and business development are often handled by a separate unit. Similarly, country risk analysis is often done by a separate unit. The larger an ECA, the better able it is to establish specialized units to handle functions such as program evaluation and development, strategic planning, management information services, communications, and separate divisions for different types of finance (such as pre-shipment guarantees, post-shipment insurance, rediscount operations, and structured project finance). Larger ECAs may also have specialized lending or guaranteeing units organized geographically or by product specialization. Some of the most important organizational characteristics demonstrated by all successful ECAs are as follows:

- A shared vision of objectives at all levels
- Good communications throughout the organization
- Sound and comprehensive information systems
- Profitable performance as a key value
- Customer-driven business orientation
- Openness to outside influences

- Willingness to undertake new projects and programs
- Strong, consistent leadership
- Commitment to recruiting the best people
- Progressive human resources development practices

Marketing, promotion, or communication departments have played a prominent role in most ECAs. The need for specialized export credits, guarantees, and insurance and the benefits these products offer are not always obvious to exporters and banks. Thus, the most successful ECAs make continuous efforts to inform prospective users about the existence of their services and encourage them to apply for assistance. As Malcolm Stephens of the Berne Union said, "It is no use simply waiting for customers to come to see the ECA. The agency must get out into the business and banking community and vigorously market its products and services."

The quality of an ECA's personnel is, of course, an important determinant of its success or failure. Intelligent, resourceful, and flexible individuals are needed at all levels of management and administration, and are most of all required at the top of the ECA organization. ECAs around the world have shown conclusively that the greatest element in success has been the personality, capabilities, and experience of the CEO. The most successful CEOs have usually had solid banking backgrounds and strong government connections. Their common sense, energy, and ability to attract and retain dedicated and skilled subordinates have been essential to the growth and profitability of their ECAs.

ECA administrative expenses vary widely for many reasons, including the general structure of wages and salaries, rents, and utility costs. Other factors affecting administrative expenses include economies of scale, the extent to which discretionary authority has been delegated to banks and exporters, and the unit size of transactions. The best way to compare administrative expenses between countries is to relate them to premium income (see Table 17.1).

Some idea of an ECA's operational efficiency can be gained by dividing the volume of business covered by the number of staff. This yields wide differences in the average value of exports handled by each staff member (see Table 17.2).

Table 17.1
Berne Union Members' Administrative Costs/Premium Income (in Percent)

1990	22.6%
1991	20.1%
1992	19.0%
1993	19.3%
1994	18.4%
1995	20.0%
1996	19.8%
1997	16.6%
1998	17.9%

Source: Berne Union.

Table 17.2
Staff Efficiency of Selected Export Credit Agencies (1995)

	Exports Supported by Agency ($mn)	Number of Staff Members	Exports Per Staff Member ($mn)
USA EXIMBANK	$9,298	126	$73.79
Australia EFIC	$2,499	84	$29.75
New Zealand EXGO	$ 563	20	$28.17
Netherlands NCM	$7,836	637	$12.30
Spain CESCE	$3,140	361	$ 8.70
Canada EDC	$1,810	562	$ 3.22

Source: Annual Reports.

NOTE

1. First Washington Associates, *A Study of Institution Building for Post-Shipment Financing, Export Credit Insurance and Guarantees to Banks in Developing Countries* (Arlington, VA: FWA, 1986), chap. V.

18

Problem Loans, Claims and Collections

The way an export credit agency (ECA) deals with claims and collections and problem loans is the ultimate determinant of its success or failure. For example, ECAs must accept that their claims and problem loans, when added to administrative expenses, will almost certainly exceed operational income in the early years of operation. In such circumstances, some ECAs (such the Foreign Credit Insurance Association syndicate in the U.S. in the 1960s) have been tempted to deny or delay paying claims. This is the worst thing that could be done because guarantee and insurance policyholders take out coverage because they expect claims to be honored in a timely fashion. Claims paid are the best advertising an ECA can have and failure to pay is the worst. In the case of FCIA, its failure to pay claims promptly stunted its growth at the outset and hindered its early efforts to obtain a large, balanced book of business—the preconditions for eventual operational success.

Even when an ECA has been in business for a long time, it may run into periods lasting a year, or even several years, when claims exceed premium income. Overreaction to temporary movements of this nature can drive exporters away from the ECA. Many ECA managers believe that all premium and claims data should be viewed in a moving five-year time frame, so that good years have a chance to outweigh bad ones, and actions are not taken in reaction to short-run phenomena that are not significant over the long run.

ECAs usually incorporate a waiting period of 90–180 days in their export credit insurance policies, during which the exporter must attempt to collect past due receivables before making claim on the ECA. This allows time for the exporter to make a full-fledged effort to collect from the borrower before turning the matter over to the ECA. ECAs' direct loans and guarantees do not usually incorporate such an extended waiting period.

The best ECAs expeditiously handle claims and recoveries efforts on past due direct loans and guaranteed credits. They are not overly technical or inflexible and do not hide behind the "fine print" or technicalities of an insurance policy to avoid paying claims. However, they do make sure that the loss was caused by a risk specified in the policy and not by an uncovered risk. For example, losses caused by an exporter's fraud or illegality may be specifically excluded under certain policies. Early collection efforts are important to establish the ECA's interest and persistence in the obligor's mind, as well as to enforce security interests or take other collateral if necessary.

Once it is established that a guarantee or insurance claim is valid, the ECA may request the claimant's permission to attempt to reschedule the loan. Otherwise, the ECA will make prompt payment to the claimant. In the case of its own direct loans, the ECA may seek to reschedule the loan or call the entire balance due and payable. In either event, the ECA will make adjustments to its reserves to account for the greater possibility of ultimate loss. The ECA's claims department will keep the underwriting department informed on all claims so that the underwriters can factor such information into their decisions on new credits. In the case of short-term credits, claims payments made by the ECA cover the agreed percentage of the entire guaranteed or insured loan. For medium- and long-term credits, the ECA may either pay the one installment in default or the entire outstanding balance of the loan.

If the decision is made to reschedule a loan that is in default for commercial reasons, the ECA normally tries to ensure the following: (1) the relief sought is necessary because the obligor cannot repay the loans as previously scheduled; (2) the relief sought will make it possible for the borrower to resume prompt payments; (3) other creditors are granting similar reschedulings; and (4) no one else is getting additional security that is better than that received by the ECA. The cause of loss is critical in influencing these and all subsequent actions taken by the ECA. If the cause is political (war, riot, revolution, expropriation, lack of foreign exchange), the ECA will pursue recoveries with both the foreign government and the obligor, whereas private buyer losses caused by commercial reasons (insolvency or protracted default) will normally involve recovery efforts solely with the borrower.

These recovery efforts will be undertaken by the ECA pursuant to its own interests as lender or under so-called subrogation rights it possesses as guarantor or insurer of the loan. In either event, the ECA tries to enforce its security rights to get paid by calling on local guarantees or collateral, if they exist, or seeks to obtain additional security that will give the ECA a preferred creditor position. Efforts are made directly or through agents to pressure the borrower into payment. In this connection, the ECA may use the services of its own staff, the insured bank or exporter, its embassy in the foreign country, local attorneys, collection agencies, or other debt recovery specialists.[1] Resort to local courts may be necessary to enforce creditors' rights, although out-of-cost settlements are pursued and preferred by most ECAs.

If the problem loan is part of a large group of similar loans in trouble—usually because of fundamental balance of payments problems and over-borrowing by the country in question—the ECA may be asked by the debtor country to reschedule all loans in question, and for this purpose, the ECA may turn to the Paris Club, an *ad hoc* organization of creditor governments and their ECAs that has met since 1956, when Argentina rescheduled its debt at a meeting chaired by the French government. The creditor group met subsequently in several different locations through the 1950s and 1960s. The rescheduling of Indonesian debt in 1970 marked the beginning of the modern Paris Club, meeting each time in Paris with the French government acting as both host and intermediary between the debtor and the creditors. In the 1980s, the Paris Club met on a frequent, nearly monthly basis. During the 1990s, fortunately for all parties, Paris Club activity decreased considerably as most developing countries improved their foreign debt situation.

The Paris Club has no charter, rules, firm membership, or legal status. It is less an organization and more a process that debtor governments follow when they are not able to meet their debt service payments. The aim of the Paris Club is to establish general principles for debt restructuring negotiations between creditor and debtor nations. Underlying all rescheduling by the Paris Club are requirements that the debtor country commit to policy and program reforms that will improve its ability to repay foreign loans. The Paris Club works in co-operation with the International Monetary Fund (IMF), the multilateral development banks, and private lenders which reschedule their loans to the country through the London Club, an *ad hoc* organization of commercial banks. The Paris Club seeks to ensure that all ECA creditors are treated the same in its countrywide reschedulings.

In the late 1990s, governments of the major industrialized countries agreed to the Heavily Indebted Poor Countries Initiative (HIPC) providing that under certain circumstances a portion of the poor countries' external debt to them could be forgiven. By the year 2000, this portion stood at 80 percent. The World Bank and the IMF also agreed that some poor countries' debt owed to them could be forgiven. Among the conditions demanded in exchange for debt forgiveness are undertakings by the debtor to adhere to financial and economic reforms and the allocation of increased domestic resources to social infrastructure, such as education and health.

Table 18.1
Berne Union Members' Recoveries/Claims (in Percent)

1990	34.2%
1991	30.3%
1992	35.7%
1993	36.6%
1994	41.2%
1995	62.0%
1996	86.1%
1997	158.0%
1998	152.8%

Source: Berne Union.

The HIPC program is intended to share more widely the debt burdens of the poor countries. The associated debt forgiveness is expected to improve the economic prospects of the poor countries.[2] In some instances, ECAs have argued successfully that because their governments have effectively frustrated ECA collection efforts, the ECA should be reimbursed by the government for its loss, even though the ECA is an agency of the government. This serves to protect the financial viability of the ECA. By the year 2000, ECA losses due to HIPC concerned only those agencies in rich countries. However, if flows of concessional finance to poor countries continue to decline, ECAs in other countries that become industrialized may be called on to participate in debt forgiveness programs.

Actual experience of ECAs with commercial risks claims down through the years has been quite good. Individual results vary, of course, but the Export-Import Bank of the United States (Eximbank) has been fairly typical in the incidence of commercial risk claims on its portfolio. In a landmark study of its claims over a twenty-five-year period, Eximbank found that commercial risk claims amounted to only about 1 percent of the insured value of exports. Of those claims, almost all were paid by Eximbank, with subsequent recovery of about 10 percent of the claims paid. In stark contrast, political risk claims (overwhelmingly due to transfer risk or lack of foreign exchange) were extremely high during the 1980s and only returned to reasonable levels in the early 1990s. However, Eximbank and other ECAs usually recover most transfer risk claims over time, so that recoveries can be 90 percent or higher over time.

Experience of Berne Union (International Union of Credit and Investment Insurers) ECAs since 1998 on both commercial and political risks reflects a drastic decline in claims and a significant increase in recoveries (see Table 18.1).

The extraordinary increase in recoveries in 1997 and 1998 is unlikely to continue much into subsequent years. In fact, it is impossible for re-coveries to exceed 100 percent of claims over a prolonged period since, by definition, recoveries represent the recapture of amounts previously paid as claims.

NOTES

1. Stephen D. Proctor, *Maximizing Recovery of Commercial Debt Claims* (Washington, DC: U.S. Eximbank, 1988), Annex A.

2. Albert Hamilton, *FWA Quarterly Newsletter, December 1999* (Arlington, VA: First Washington Associates, 1999), 5.

19

Results of Operations

The two most important indexes of export credit agencies' (ECAs) operational success are the amount of exports they support and their financial results (which determine their ability to continue to finance a
substantial volume of exports). The Berne Union (International Union of
Credit and Investment Insurers) members, which include some of the
world's largest ECAs, have shown a general increase in the value of
exports they supported since 1990,[1] but this increase has been less than
the rise in value of their nations' total exports. As a consequence, exports
supported by Berne Union members have slowly changed from about
12 percent of their national exports in 1990–1991 to about 9 percent in
1999 (see Table 19.1)

At the same time that Berne Union members, particularly those in
Organization for Economic Co-operation and Development (OECD)
countries, financed a falling percentage of national exports, non-Berne
Union ECAs financed growing percentages of their nations' exports. Calculations by First Washington Associates (FWA) in 2000 indicated that
exports covered by all of the world's ECAs (Berne Union and non-Berne
Union) amounted to about 12 percent of total global exports.

During the decade of the 1990s, while their export support was growing in dollar terms (but falling as a percent of national exports), Berne
Union members showed a complete turnaround in their financial results
(see Table 19.2). Between 1990 and 1995, aggregate net losses of the members of the union declined from $7.2 billion to $0.5 billion. In 1996, for
the first time in a decade, the members showed an aggregate profit of

Table 19.1
Exports Supported by Berne Union Members (US$ billion)

	Exports Supported	Total National Exports	Exports Supported/ Total National Exports
1990	328.6	2,845.5	11.5%
1991	349.9	2,962.5	11.8%
1992	360.6	3,165.8	11.4%
1993	344.1	3,151.4	10.9%
1994	375.5	3,658.8	10.3%
1995	383.2	4,337.7	8.8%
1996	406.7	4,481.0	9.1%
1997	350.6	4,573.4	7.7%
1998	379.0	4,615.0	8.2%
1999	411.0	4,680.1	8.8%

Source: Berne Union and International Monetary Fund (IMF).

Table 19.2
Net Annual Results of Berne Union Members (US$ billions)

	(LOSS)	PROFIT
1990	(7.2)	
1991	(6.2)	
1992	(5.2)	
1993	(6.1)	
1994	(6.3)	
1995	(0.5)	
1996		0.5
1997		6.1
1998		5.6
1999		3.0

Source: Berne Union.

about $0.5 billion. In 1997 and 1998, annual profits exceeded $5 billion, and in 1999, profits were $3.0 billion. Berne Union officials attributed this welcome development to higher premium levels, lower claims payments, and improved recovery experience.

As of the end of 1998, the Berne Union members as a group still had a cumulative deficit from prior years, but twenty-two of the total of forty-four members had cumulative surpluses, and the trend was clearly in the direction of more and more members joining those who were already cumulatively profitable since inception of their operations. Non-Berne Union members as a group have a more consistent record of surpluses—reflecting the private sector ownership of many of them and the requirements for financial soundness imposed by their shareholders and/or governments.[2]

NOTES

1. International Union of Credit and Investment Insurers, *The Berne Union 1999 Yearbook* (London, England: Berne Union, 1999), 164.

2. First Washington Associates, *Special Report on International Competitiveness* (Arlington, VA: FWA, 1998), 163–167.

20

Political Risk Evaluation

Expert credit agencies (ECAs) attempt to evaluate the probability that political events will affect economic systems in ways that will impede repayment of external obligations. For this purpose, ECAs have adopted country risk evaluation systems that typically blend objective and subjective analyses of individual aspects of risk and utilize various sources of information to produce a single credit rating for each country. This information is then incorporated into a country limitation schedule that contains information about the ECA's policy of coverage for all countries in the world. The main political risks assumed by ECAs include the following factors. Different countries present greater or lesser political risks in each of these categories, depending on their background, history, cultural factors, political system, and many other factors.

Commercial Risks of Public Buyers

   1. Insolvency of the buyer (or guarantor)
   2. Protracted default

Regular Political Risks

   1. War risks—War, civil war, rebellion, revolution, insurrection, and civil commotion
   2. Government intervention—requisition, expropriation, confiscation, or intervention into the business of the buyer or guarantor by a governmental authority
   3. Export embargo

a. cancellation of export license

b. nonrenewal of export license

c. imposition of restrictions on the export, as they relate to the products, service, or equipment and materials necessary to render the services, not due to the fault of the buyer

4. Import imbargo

a. cancellation of import license or authority

b. imposition of any law, order, decree, regulation having force of law or any other government action of like nature that prevents the import, as they relate to the products, service, or equipment and materials necessary to render the services, not due to the fault of the buyer

5. Conversion and transfer risks

a. inability to obtain foreign exchange in a lawful market and to effect transfer to the exporter of local currency deposited in a local bank or designated depository within ninety days of the due date, not due to the fault of the buyer

b. Imposition of any law, order, decree or regulation having the force of law which prevents the local currency deposit

Most European ECAs establish a maximum limit for outstanding loans, guarantees, and insurance per country) at least for the most difficult markets. All private export credit insurers do so, based upon the requirements of their reinsurers. For some ECAs in North America and in many developing countries, there are no formal individual country limits, but large transactions are handled on a case-by-case, in very risky countries.

Different country risk analysis systems are used by different ECAs, but most of them produce similar country ratings, which are further harmonized by regular exchanges of information among the ECAs. ECAs typically divide foreign markets into several categories for the purpose of country risk evaluation. Five widely accepted definitions of individual country risk ratings are explained here, along with some basic guidelines for assigning those ratings.[1]

Rating A: Negligible risk. Countries with this rating have solid political and social institutions, well-developed economies, and capital markets that are integrated with, and central to, the world economy. Problems facing these nations do not threaten political and economic stability. The "A" countries are found largely among the Organization for Economic Cooperation and Development (OECD) group of nations.

Rating B: Relatively little risk. Most of these nations possess well-established political and social institutions and developed economies. They, however, are somewhat more peripheral to global financial markets, more borrower than lender, and may incur persistent current account deficits. Debt burdens range from light to substantial but are easily manageable given diversified access to capital markets. Also included are those developing countries with very favorable net external asset positions and stable, though relatively less developed, political and economic environments.

Rating C: Some risk. Countries with this rating present a high probability of uninterrupted debt servicing. They do not face any immediate threat to orderly servicing of their external debt but possess some weaknesses that could lead to a deterioration in debt servicing capacity. Countries so rated tend to be relatively stable, developing nations with workable political mechanisms. They are, however, likely to face problems with social integration, economic, and political development or possible external threats because of their geographic location. Debt service burdens are relatively heavy, though managed without much difficulty. Countries so rated should have the capacity to adjust reasonably well to external shocks.

Rating D: Significant risk. External debt in these countries is expected to be serviced, at least in the near future. Domestic resource mobilization is likely to be limited, while ties to world financial markets are few and tenuous. The external position is likely to be weak. The country may be a substantial net borrower, face a large debt service burden relative to repayment capacity, and possess a weak net international liquidity position. Political institutions may be weak to nonexistent, sociocultural factors adverse, and the level of economic development limited. Dependence on primary commodities is likely to be substantial. In some cases, actual or potential political instability is present, limiting the government's ability to undertake effective policies. Many of these countries have rescheduled their external debts at least once and face persistent balance of payment problems and shortage of foreign exchange. Some will need to reschedule additional maturities in the medium term, but economic adjustment will have progressed sufficiently to envision the nation returning to more normal status on world capital markets.

Off Cover: Cannot, or are unlikely to be able to, service their external obligations as originally contracted. Ties to world financial markets are very limited, and these countries face serious problems due to a lack of political integration, poor economic performance, heavy debt burdens, and/or intense social conflict that are expected to prevent the normal servicing of external liabilities. Some of these countries appear to function well on a day-to-day basis, but the underlying severity of their situation will generate the potential for serious challenges to the ruling elite over time. Countries with this rating have deteriorated to the point where the probability of anything more than token interest payments is extremely low in the near future. These nations usually have significant interest arrearages that adversely affect the accrual status of loans outstanding, have consistently failed to comply with International Monetary Fund (IMF) or other adjustment programs, and show no definite prospects for an early restoration of debt service.

In the late 1990s, the OECD developed a new country risk evaluation system designed to harmonize the practices of ECAs in the industrial countries. The new OECD country risk schedule contains seven, not five, categories. Table 20.1 shows how one ECA categorized its foreign markets according to the OECD schedule in September 2000.

Country ratings do not tell the whole story of ECAs' willingness to do business in certain markets, particularly in the riskier countries and for medium- and long-term transactions. ECAs often impose restrictions that sharply limit the availability of their financial services.[2] The Export-Import Bank of the United States (Eximbank) makes an annual evaluation of ECA's real willingness to cover transactions for countries around the world. For this purpose, Eximbank analyzes the policies of ECAs in Germany, France, Canada, the United States, Japan, and Italy. In Eximbank's own case, for example, they were off cover (i.e., would not cover transactions) for about 15 percent of the world's countries in 1999, had significant restrictions on covering an additional 25 percent of the countries, and moderate restrictions on a further 15 percent. In only about 45 percent of the markets, the U.S. Eximbank was open to cover transactions without restrictions,) despite the fact that they considered themselves to be the most forthcoming of the ECAs studied (see Table 20.2).

Internal and external political situations are very important to ECAs as they assess country risk. Wars, riots, revolutions, and civil unrest proceed from unstable political situations. Some objective data are available to analyze these types of risks, such as numbers of border incidents, bombings, terrorist killings, strikes, and violent demonstrations. However, most judgments about these types of risks are heavily subjective. The political situation and the economic-financial position cannot be easily separated, as each affects the other.

One approach used by ECAs to determine the economic-financial position of countries is to define a number of indicators and assign a weight to them. For example, Table 20.3 assigns equal weight to nine major economic-financial indicators for each country. The indicators selected are good ones for the purpose of determining the country's ability to repay foreign obligations in a timely fashion. Indicators 4–9 deal with the country's external balance of payments, and indicators 1–3 are reflective of internal economic policy and welfare, which are related to, or can produce changes, which will ultimately affect the country's debt servicing capacity.

Another approach included in some ECA country risk evaluation systems is an analysis of relations with the International Monetary Fund

Table 20.1
Belgium's Official Export Credit Agency: Short-term Country Risk Table

Country	Risk	Country	Risk	Country	Risk	Country	Risk
Afghanistan	7	Djibouti	4	Libya	2	Rwanda	6
Albania	6	Dominica	5	Liechtenstein	1	Samoa, American	2
Algeria	4	Dominican Republic	5	Lithuania	4	Samoa (Western)	4
Andorra	1	Ecuador	6	Luxembourg	1	San Marino	1
Angola	7	Egypt	2	Macau	2	Sao Tome & Principe	7
Anguilla	5	El Salvador	3	Macedonia	6	Saudi Arabia	3
Antigua & Barbuda	3	Equatorial Guinea	4	Madagascar	6	Senegal	4
Argentina	4	Eritrea	5	Madeira Islands	1	Seychelles	7
Armenia	5	Estonia	3	Malawi	4	Sierra Leone	7
Aruba (Netherlands)	2	Ethiopia	5	Malaysia	1	Singapore	1
Australia	1	Faeroe Islands	1	Maldives	3	Slovakia	4
Austria	1	Falkland Islands	2	Mali	4	Slovenia	1
Azerbaijan	5	Fiji	2	Malta	3	Solomon Islands	6
Azores	1	Finland	1	Man (Isle of)	1	Somalia	7
Bahamas	4	France	1	Mariana Islands (N.)	2	South Africa	4
Bahrain	2	French Guyana	1	Marshall Islands	6	Spain	1
Bangladesh	4	French Polynesia	2	Martinique	1	Sri Lanka	3
Barbados	2	Gabon	4	Mauritania	6	St. Helena	2
Belarus	7	Gambia	4	Mauritius	3	St. Kitts Nevis	3
Belgium	1	Georgia	6	Mayotte	2	St. Lucia	3
Belize	6	Germany	1	Mexico	3	St. Pierre & Miquelon	2
Benin	4	Ghana	5	Micronesia	5	St. Vincent & Grenadines	5
Bermuda	2	Gibraltar	1	Moldova	6	Sudan	7
Bhutan	3	Greece	2	Monaco	1	Suriname	7
Bolivia	5	Greenland	1	Mongolia	5	Swaziland	2
Bosnia Herzegovina	6	Grenada	5	Montserrat	4	Sweden	1
Botswana	1	Guadeloupe	1	Morocco	2	Switzerland	1
Brazil	4	Guam	2	Mozambique	5	Syria	5
Brunei	1	Guatemala	5	Myanmar	5	Taiwan	1
Bulgaria	2	Guinea Bissau	4	Namibia	3	Tajikistan	7
Burkina Faso	4	Guinea Republic	5	Nauru	4	Tanzania	4
Burundi	6	Guyana	4	Nepal	2	Thailand	3
Cambodia	6	Haiti	6	Netherlands	1	Togo	4
Cameroon	4	Honduras	4	Netherlands Antilles	3	Tokelau	5
Canada	1	Hong Kong	1	New Caledonia	2	Tonga	4
Canary Islands	1	Hungary	2	New Zealand	1	Trinidad & Tobago	4
Cape Verde Islands	6	Iceland	1	Nicaragua	6	Tunisia	3
Cayman Islands	2	India	2	Niger	4	Turkey	4
Central African Republic	4	Indonesia	5	Nigeria	6	Turkmenistan	7
Ceuta & Melilla	2	Iran	4	Niue	3	Turks and Caicos	2
Chad	4	Iraq	7	Norfolk	2	Tuvalu	5
Channel Island	1	Ireland	1	Norway	1	Uganda	3
Chile	3	Israel	3	Oman	4	Ukraine	5
China	1	Italy	1	Pakistan	6	United Arab Emirates	3
Christmas Island	1	Jamaica	4	Palau	2	United Kingdom	1
Colombia	3	Japan	1	Palestine	7	United States of America	1
Comoros	4	Jordan	3	Panama	3	Uruguay	2
Congo (formerly Zaire)	7	Kazakhstan	5	Papua New Guinea	5	Uzbekistan	5
Congo (The Republic)	7	Kenya	5	Paraguay	3	Vanuatu	5
Cook Islands	2	Kiribati	2	Peru	4	Vatican City	1
Coral Sea Islands	1	Korea (North)	7	Philippines	2	Venezuela	3
Costa Rica	3	Korea (South)	2	Pitcairn Island	2	Vietnam	4
Cote d'Ivoire	4	Kuwait	3	Poland	1	Virgin Islands (U.S.A.)	2
Croatia	3	Kyrgyzstan	5	Portugal	1	Virgin Islands (U.K.)	2
Cuba	7	Laos	5	Puerto Rico	2	Wallis & Futuna Islands	2
Cyprus (South/Greek)	3	Latvia	4	Qatar	4	Western Sahara	3
Cyprus (north/Turkish)	5	Lebanon	4	Reunion	1	Yemen	4
Czech Republic	2	Lesotho	4	Romania	5	Yugoslavia	7
Denmark	1	Liberia	7	Russia	5	Zambia	6
						Zimbabwe	6

Notes: 1 = Lowest Political Risk, 7 = Highest Political Risk.

Source: Ducroire/Delcredere of Belgium.

Table 20.2
Comparison of Medium- and Long-Term ECA Country Cover Policy

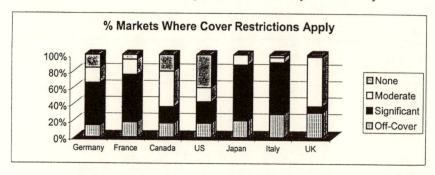

(IMF), World Bank (IBRD), and other international institutions. This can be used to prepare the following risk categories:

A	Not eligible for IBRD assistance because of advanced state of economy
B	In good position with IBRD/IMF but makes small use because of good economy
C	Eligible for IBRD/IMF programs; relatively frequent user
D	Eligible for IBRD/IMF programs, particularly International Development Association implementing agreed reform measurers
E	Ineligible to receive IBRD/IMF programs because of past performance, unwillingness to commit to corrective measures
Off Cover	Difficulties in payment, unable to reach agreement with IMF and lack of structural adjustment program; Bank has suspended previously approved credits

A number of private services provide information about countries and make evaluations of country risks.[3] Many of these services' findings are utilized by the ECAs. The private services do extensive analyses of political, economic, financial, and commercial conditions in borrowing countries. Most of them provide narrative descriptions of country conditions, emphasizing what the service believes are the most important factors to be weighed in determining country risk. In addition, in most cases, the countries are rated and/or ranked as to relative risk. Professional country risk services are offered by Bank of America, Business Environment Risk Intelligence, Control Risks Group, Frost & Sullivan, International Country Risk Guide, Euromoney, Institutional Investor, Economist Intelligence Unit, Political Risk Services, and S. J. Rundt &

Table 20.3
Indicators of Economic-Financial Position

Indicator		"A"	"B"	"C"	"D"	Off Cover
			Category			
1. Annual Growth of per capita GDP	1/ 4/	Greater than 3.1	3.0 - 2.1	2.0 - 1.1	Less than 1.0	Negative
2. Inflation Rate	1/ 4/	Less than 6	7 - 25	26 - 50	51 - 75	Greater than 76
3. Budget/GDP	1/ 4/	Surplus	Deficit Up to 5.0	Deficit of 5.1 to 10	Deficit of 10.1 to 15	Deficit more than 15.1
4. Current Account Balance	1/ 4/	Surplus	Deficit Up to 5.0	Deficit of 5.1 to 10	Deficit of 10.1 to 15	Deficit more than 15.1
5. External Debt Exports	1/ 4/	Up to 50.0	50.1 to 100	100.1 to 150	150.1 to 200	More than 200.1
6. External Debt/ GDP	1/ 4/	Up to 25.0	25.1 to 50.0	50.1 to 75.0	75.11 to 100	More than 100.1
7. Debt Service/Exports	1/ 4/	Up to 5.0	5.1 to 10.0	10.1 to 20.0	20.11 to 30.0	More than 30.1
8. F/X Reserves/Imports (Months)	1/	More than 4.1	3.10 to 4.00	1.10 to 3.00	1.10 to 2.00	Less than 1.0
9. Payment Delays/ Debt Service	1/ 3/	0	0	0.01 to 0.25		0.25 to 0.50More than 0.50

Notes: 1/Average of the last three years; 2/Consumer price index, average of the last three years; 3/Last six months; 4/Expressed in percentage.

Associates. Moody's and Standard & Poor provide some of the most helpful analyses of the creditworthiness of foreign government entities, which are frequently incorporated by the ECAs in their own evaluations of country creditworthiness.

NOTES

1. These rating definitions are an amalgam of developing country ECA sources.

2. United Nations Conference on Trade and Development, *Trade and Development Report, 1997* (Geneva, Switzerland: UNCTAD, 1997), 39–41.

3. Llewellyn D. Howell, *The Handbook of Country and Political Risk Analysis*, 2d ed. East Syracuse, NY: The PRS Group, 1998), 3–10.

21

Commercial Risk Evaluation

Export credit agencies (ECAs) use many different methods for evaluating the commercial risks of transactions they cover. These risks are of two types: (1) bankruptcy or insolvency and (2) delays in payment for other reasons. For the minority of business that is medium to long term, most ECAs will make a detailed analysis of financial projections including income statements, funds flow forecasts, and balance sheets for the entire period of the loan, backed by market evaluations, engineering studies, and economic information. For the large majority of cases, which are short term, however, ECAs generally rely on credit reports and other information submitted by the exporter on the buyer's creditworthiness and reliability. A number of independent credit information services exist in both industrial and developing countries, which are utilized by the ECAs.[1] Also, ECAs frequently offer credit information to others on firms that are located in their own countries. Some of the most important elements addressed in ECAs' commercial risk assessments are explained here.[2]

1. *What is the exporter's prior experience with the buyer?* The ECA's own files are first checked to determine what past experience the ECA has had with the buyer. This is important to determine the total potential exposure for the ECA, including the application under consideration. Negative information and experience signal caution, and good experience helps to support granting of additional coverage. The underwriter also checks to see that the information in the files is consistent with the credit limit application under consideration.

2. What is the exporters prior experience with the buyer? This is a very important element in assessing a buyer. If the exporter has been successfully trading with a buyer for some time and for amounts similar to that requested in the credit limit application, this is a very strong indication that the buyer is likely to continue to pay the exporter. Good past payment experience is probably the best indicator of future prompt payment. Also, in many cases, an exporter has a great deal of information about a buyer and the buyer's business, which could be useful in making a decision on a credit limit. This information can be particularly useful where there is difficulty in making a recommendation. The information provided by the exporter is usually compared and weighed against the information from other sources.

3. How long has the buyer been operating? The length of time a business has been in operation is an important element in assessing the creditworthiness of a buyer. Certain presumptions are made regarding a company that has been in business for a number of years and has traded effectively in that period of time. If there is no information to the contrary for experienced, long-established firms, the ECA normally presumes that the business has effective management, is likely to have an acceptable record of payment of its creditors, and is in an industry sufficiently stable to allow for viable business operations. When a company has been recently established, greater care is exercised in credit assessment, especially on such matters as adequate capitalization, and quality and experience of management.

4. Are the buyer's directors and senior managers experienced and successful? Quality of management is a critical element to the success of a business, particularly in industries and economies where there is open competition requiring effective management for survival. Accordingly, ECA underwriters focus on the identity of the managers and their experience. If there is new, unproven management combined with adverse recent developments, caution is exercised in approving a credit limit.

5. Have any recent changes in management or ownership occurred? If so, what is the impact? Where there have been recent major changes in senior management, greater care is exercised by the ECA in making presumptions based on the previous trading history of the company. An attempt is normally made to obtain information on the experience and track record of the new management. Where there has been a recent change in ownership, care is taken to ascertain whether there has been an adverse change in the policy of the company, such as increased borrowing, higher debt/equity ratio, extended payment terms from creditors, and higher dividend payments.

6. Is the buyer diversified or reliant on one or two products? If reliant on one or two products, where is the business cycle now? Many industries are subject to business cycles that can cause high levels of bankruptcies, such as the building industry or trading in some types of commodities. The ECA tries to keep in touch with the stage of the business cycle and the fortunes of those engaged in the industry concerned.

7. *Is there any significant history of overdue payment?* This is a critical element in underwriting short-term credit risk. If there is a history of defaults and/or long delays in payment of debts, particularly trade debts, cover is denied unless there is a justifiable reason for believing that past behavior will not be a reliable guide to the future. Justifiable reasons might be a change of ownership or management to persons with a sound record of operating or managing organizations that honor their commercial debts, or a substantial injection of funds into an organization that has been operating with less than acceptable levels of working capital. Any company with a recent history of defaults or lengthy overdue payments is normally denied approval. In some cases where there is an established pattern of overdue payments without outright defaults, approval with a longer than usual period to pay claims may be considered as an underwriting condition on approval. Little regard is usually given to any claims by the exporter that a special relationship exists between the exporter and the buyer, implying that payment of the debt to the exporter would be favored over other debts.

8. *Is working capital adequate?* The adequacy of working capital is a critical issue for underwriting short-term credit insurance. A company may have a number of longer-term problems, such as a higher than appropriate debt level or gradual decline in profitability. These will be of major concern to an investor or long-term lender and will ultimately be reflected in a shortfall of working capital. These matters are not as critical to a short-term insurer as is adequacy of working capital. Working capital is defined as current assets minus current liabilities. Current assets are cash, accounts receivables and stocks. Current liabilities are accounts payable and debts maturing in the short term, that is, within a period of twelve months. Working capital determines whether a company can meet its immediate or current debts as they fall due. The adequacy of working capital is determined by means of the current ratio, which is current assets divided by current liabilities. Clearly a company with less readily realizable assets than immediately payable debts cannot be an acceptable credit risk unless there is evidence of external support by shareholders, directors, or the buyer's bank. What is a desirable ratio is open to question. Generally speaking, a current ratio of 1.5 to 1 is regarded as healthy by ECAs. Underwriters, however, encounter buyers with less acceptable ratios than this and may approve credit limits for these buyers if the totality of information indicates that this is not a serious problem. One useful guide is to have regard to the industry average if this information is available.

9. *Is the buyer profitable?* Since ECAs are normally concerned with prof-

itability from the point of view of a short-term trade creditor, the most important thing underwriters check is whether the buyer is profitable and there is not a significant trend of declining profitability. Two relevant indicators are return on sales (net profit after tax divided by net sales) and return on assets (net profit after tax divided by total assets). It is difficult to determine what is an acceptable level of profit from the perspective of short-term credit risk. Regard is normally paid to the industry average, if available. It is not satisfactory if a company has been making large recent losses unless the reason is clear and short-lived and reserves are sufficient to allow continued trading. In cases where there is declining profitability or actual losses being incurred, but the company is considered good for a short-term transaction, credit approvals are sometimes limited in time to allow an early review to take place.

10. Is net worth satisfactory? The net worth is the total assets of the company minus the total liabilities. It represents the amount available to shareholders of the company and the amount available to finance losses. The bigger the proportion of net worth to total assets, the greater the buffer against ultimate insolvency. However, before too much reliance is placed on net worth, the quality of the assets and the ability of the company to convert the assets into cash with which to pay short-term creditors are examined. Credit limits are not approved based solely on net worth when it appears that the company is in financial difficulties, particularly if there is some doubt about the quality or liquidity of the assets.

11. Is the buyer in an expansion, contraction, or steady phase? If the business is rapidly expanding, certain elements of the company's recent history are carefully checked. Overly rapid expansion can be dangerous if the resources of the company are being pushed to the limit. The most important element to be concerned with for an expanding company is the position and trend of the working capital. Other elements that are checked are profitability, debt service, and debt/equity relationships. A company with a history of operating profitably and effectively at a steady rate is clearly a good credit risk. If the business is contracting, ECAs are concerned about the quality of management and the external economic factors impinging upon the trading operations of the buyer, such as deregulation increasing the level of competition in the buyer's industry or the stage of the business cycle of the buyer's industry. To determine the trend of a company, analysis of several years' financial statements is undertaken. This is done if the size of the business warrants this approach and there are indications that such an analysis would yield useful results.

12. Are borrowings within safe limits and appropriately structured? Has there been any change in the debt profile of the business? This can be determined by looking at the buyer's debt/equity ratio (total debt divided by shareholders equity). To determine the significance of the debt/equity ratio, it may be necessary to refer to the industry average. Some industries such as banks and financial institutions have apparently high debt/equity ratios, but this is due to the nature of the business. There is a general principle that for a manufacturing or trading company, it is appropriate to have a debt/equity ratio of not more than 2:1. If this rule were strictly applied, the practical necessity of approving credit limits would be overlooked. If the debt/equity ratio is higher than the industry average, other important factors such as levels of working capital and the debt servicing record are normally scrutinized. Debt that is appropriately structured allows for debt servicing at times best suited to the debtor's cash flows and within affordable limits. ECA underwriters frequently encounter situations where the buyer is dependent on short-term overdraft facilities for survival, whereas the appropriate structure would be long-term debt. The buyers in these situations can be entirely dependent on the bank's goodwill in rolling over short-term facilities. In these cases, the ECA must exercise extra discretion and judgment. Many companies trade continuously on these terms, and it would not be realistic to refuse a credit limit based solely on this fact. In cases where this situation exists and there appear to be deteriorating financial circumstances, the ECA may require that the buyer provide written indications of continued support from the bank, before deciding on a recommendation. A recent change from medium-term amortized debt to short-term securities or a sudden increase in loans to or by directors or shareholders are examples of situations that may need to be explained before a credit limit is recommended for approval.

13. *Are there any negative elements such as disputes, court proceedings or political events adversely affecting the buyer or the buyer's markets?* This item reminds underwriters to be conscious of events or circumstances that might have an impact on the buyer's ability to pay. Disputes, court proceedings, or government actions seriously impacting the borrower are almost always investigated thoroughly by the ECA to determine whether they pose a threat to payment of trade-related indebtedness.

14. *Is the quality of the credit report high and does it recommend a transaction of this size and payment terms?* The underwriter tries to ascertain whether the quality of the information in the report is high or is largely a record of unsubstantiated assertions by the buyer's owners or managers. The quality of the report depends to some extent on the source of the information, particularly if there is good quality independent verification of the buyer's payment record. There should be good reasons, clearly explained, for going against a negative recommendation in a credit report. However, when the quality of the report is low and other information is available, a recommendation, particularly a positive one, may be disregarded.

22

Premiums and Reserves

Premiums and reserves are closely related topics for export credit agencies (ECAs) because the overall level of premiums must be sufficient to cover related operational costs, including setting aside reserves that are sufficient to pay related claims. Most new ECAs depend upon the experience of their counterparts as a guide to the initial levels of premiums and reserves they should establish. Then, as they gain experience, ECAs adjust premiums and reserves to achieve long-term goals of maintaining the real value of the capital base.

PREMIUM COMPONENTS

In order to achieve the objective of self-sufficiency and full cost recovery, premiums are designed to cover commissions, net political risks losses, net commercial risk losses, administrative expenses, and a profit margin for the ECA (see Figure 22.1). A number of factors influence the premiums charged by ECAs for export credit insurance.[1] The main ones are discussed here.

Pricing Philosophy. Although this term can mean several things, here it is taken to mean whether or not an export credit insurance system is based on the principle of self sufficiency. Most agencies are, but sometimes with a division between those transactions that should theoretically pay for themselves and those transactions that are for a "national account."

Whole Turnover or Spread-of-Risk Requirements. Many countries offer

Figure 22.1
The Basic Fee Model

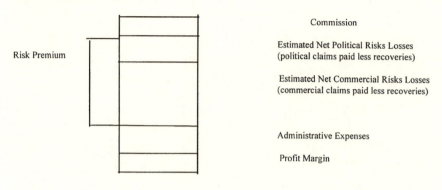

Commission

Estimated Net Political Risks Losses
(political claims paid less recoveries)

Estimated Net Commercial Risks Losses
(commercial claims paid less recoveries)

Administrative Expenses

Profit Margin

Risk Premium

short-term insurance with the provision that the insured offer whole turnover or a reasonable spread-of-risk for coverage. This implies that the fees charged will be lower than if the transactions were individually selected for coverage.

Breadth and Scope of the Agency's Total Exposure. The requirement of self-sufficiency can imply much higher fees for those agencies that have most of their risks concentrated in one or two markets or products. The implication is that it is much easier for Japan's Export Insurance Division (EID) to break even from year to year with fees set at a reasonable level than it is for the Export-Import Bank of the United States (U.S. Eximbank), simply by virtue of the fact that Eximbank insures approximately 3 percent of U.S. exports whereas EID insures over 30 percent of Japan's exports. This is especially true since the U.S. Eximbank's exposure is highly concentrated in one area—Latin America.

Retention of Risk, Deductibles, Discounts. The amount of the commercial and political risk that must be retained by the exporter (and/or bank) has a very important impact on the appropriate level of fees. An exporter would probably pay a lot more for 90 percent coverage of commercial risks, as is offered by the U.S. Eximbank, than it would for 60 percent coverage, which is often offered by Japan's EID. Similarly, the impact of deductible requirements or options, heavy discounting of base rates, and other similar items all have an important bearing on fee levels.

Application Fee, Underwriting Fee. Some agencies, such as Hermes of Germany, ECGD of the United Kingdom, U.S. Eximbank, and SACE of Italy charge fees additional to the basic premium charge.

Risks Covered. Fees will vary with the type of risks that are covered, such as pre-shipment, post-shipment or combined; or political, commercial, or combined. Furthermore, each agency may define its risks

Table 22.1
Berne Union Members, 1998: Export Credit Insurance and Guarantees Premium Income As Percentage of Exports Covered

Region	Premium / Exports covered
Africa	0.7%
Asia, East	1.5%
Asia, North	0.8%
Asia, South	0.5%
Australia / New Zealand	0.5%
Europe, East	1.5%
Europe, West	1.7%
Latin America / Carribean	1.6%
Middle East	0.6%
United States / Canada	1.6%
ALL REGIONS	1.0%

Source: Annual Reports.

differently. For instance, until recently, Hermes did not cover protracted default for many transactions.

Other Criteria. Additional criteria frequently used by ECAs in determining specific fees include the credit term (tenor) involved, the country of the buyer, the buyer's financial status, the type of product to be exported, the existence of foreign competition, the existence of a guarantee from a sovereign or financial institution, experience with the exporter, and type of trade documentation utilized.

Bearing in mind the numerous factors affecting premium levels, the average premium rates for all business covered by Berne Union (International Union of Credit and Investment Insurers) members are shown in Table 22.1.

RISK MANAGEMENT AND THE ROLE OF FEES

It is important to remember that ECAs use fees mainly as a tool for controlling profitability and *not* as a tool for managing risk. The level and structure of fees depends on program objectives, the market to be serviced, and the level and differentiation of risks within that market. Despite the fact that fees should be set in accordance with the desired level of profitability, they also can be lowered to meet competition or to increase program demand.

An ECA may be thought of as originally having a large potential market demand for its services. This market is then reduced in accordance with program objectives and requirements. For instance, the potential market will be reduced by filtering out applications for the most risky transactions as undesirable for cover, as well as by considering limits on risk concentration (in certain countries, industries). It is at this point that fees should be set that will determine the level of profitability for the program.

An ECA's risk reduction system should attempt to narrow the potential book of business to those transactions with "reasonable assurance of repayment." The underlying philosophy is that risks should be standardized by underwriting criteria over broad categories in order to allow standard fees, which are differentiated only by broad categories. Although fees could be levied case by case on transactions that do not conform to underwriting standards, this would be administratively expensive and would lend itself to greater subjectivity.

The risk reduction system should consist of several tools, including use of a Country Limitation Schedule (CLS). The CLS can screen out unacceptable risk by turning away applications to risky markets entirely, or by severely limiting the credit terms that will be acceptable, such as requiring that transactions have specific guarantors or be conducted under letters of credit. A second risk reduction tool is the requirement that a certain portion of the risk be retained by the exporter for its own account. Exporter retention of 10 percent of the commercial risk of a transaction is standard. The requirement of greater risk retention should cause applicants to be wary about what transactions they submit for coverage, since they will have to share more heavily in any resulting loss. A third risk reduction tool is credit underwriting, by which the loan officer determines whether a transaction is creditworthy according to standard criteria. The loan officer may require additional special conditions, securities, or guarantees before determining that "reasonable assurance of repayment" exists.

Given the potential book of business that results after the riskiest transactions have been screened out by underwriting and other risk reduction tools, the fees selected will help determine what the actual book of business will be. Lower levels of fees will result in more applications for insurance and an overall better book of business as far as risks go. This is because the lower fees make it worthwhile for applicants to insure their less risky business as well as more risky business. On the other hand, a higher level of fees will limit the amount of business to a smaller volume of just the riskier business.

If the risks being covered vary greatly, from very risky to almost no risk, then a fee system that does not differentiate between the risk will probably suffer from the insurance problem of "moral hazard." This is the situation where less risky transactions are forced to subsidize more risky transactions. Exporters may respond by seeking no insurance for their least risky transactions. This will cause the additional low risk transactions to leave the pool and the remaining pool will require higher fees again to break even. This process will repeat itself until (or unless) the least risky transactions find subsidizing the highly risky transactions preferable to the alternative, which may be no insurance. On the other hand, if fees are adequately differentiated, there is no reason why the size of the book of business being serviced cannot be increased or decreased (within limits) and some reasonable level of profitability maintained.

RESERVES

Most ECAs are required to reserve amounts estimated to be sufficient to cover all claims and nonpayments on loans. This is often done by allocating a specific percentage of gross income or net income to statutory reserves, supplemented by case reserves for individual transactions that are deemed likely to result in a claim or nonpayment in the near future. These provisions for reserves are treated like an expense on the income statement. For those ECAs whose incomes are taxable, the effect of reserving is to reduce taxes payable on current earnings.

Many analysts claim that ECAs cannot use actuarial methods to estimate probability of nonpayment. They believe that statistics on past performance are no guide to future loan problems and claims. In their opinion, reserving must remain essentially arbitrary—dependent upon fixed formulas—plus case reserves for reported problems and incurred but not yet reported difficulties known to the ECA.

In the early 1990s, the U.S. Eximbank and a few other ECAs adopted a new method of assessing risks and establishing reserves, called the "market yield" approach.[2] This is based upon the risk evaluation of foreign countries done by private capital markets. Eximbank looks specifically at the yields on different sovereign country bonds and how Moody's and Standard & Poor (S&P) rate those bonds. The difference in yields serves as an estimate of the differing probabilities of non-payment. Eximbank's first eight country categories corresponded in a real sense to Moody's and S&P's categories as shown in Table 22.2. Eximbank's categories 9, 10, and 11 had no counterpart in Moody's and S&P because they were very risky markets where international bond issues are not usually possible.

Eximbank's estimate of losses (and the amount they reserved) was based upon risk yields in the private capital markets for the first eight categories and Eximbank's own estimates of higher losses in the last three categories based upon their actual experience as shown in Table

Table 22.2
Comparison of Country Ratings of Moody's, S&P, and U.S. Eximbank

MOODY'S	STANDARD & POOR'S	U.S. EXIMBANK
Aa	AA	1
A	A	2
AVERAGE OF A & Baa	or A & BBB	3
Baa	BBB	4
Ba	BB	5
133% OF Ba	133% OF BB	6
B	B	7
150% OF B	150% OF B	8

22.3. Risk levels 1–3 correspond to some other ECAs' "A" market rating. Risk levels 4–6 compare to a "B" market. Risk levels 7 and 8 correspond to "C" markets, and 9 and 10 match "D" markets. Risk level 11 is equivalent to "off-cover."

It is worth noting that ECAs can usually charge a premium that will meet related claims for "A" and "B" markets. This gets more difficult for "C" markets and close to impossible for "D" markets since most exporters and banks are unwilling to pay a risk premium much over 5 percent per annum. As a result, premiums lower than the amounts indicated on Table 22.3 may be charged for the riskier markets and what happens, in effect, is that the less risky business pays for the more risky business.

Table 22.3
U.S. Eximbank Estimate of Losses by Country Risk Level

Risk Level	Expected Loss		
	Long-Term	**Medium-Term**	**Short-Term**
1	1.5%	1.0%	0.2%
2	2.5%	1.55	0.3%
3	5.0%	2.5%	0.8%
4	10.0%	5.0%	1.5%
5	15.0%	10.0%	2.5%
6	20.0%	15.0%	3.5%
7	30.0%	20.0%	5.5%
8	40.0%	30.0%	8.0%
9	55.0%	40.0%	12.5%
10	65.0%	55.0%	17.0%
11	75.0%	65.0%	25.0%

NOTES

1. Many of these premium-setting concepts are embodied in internal staff papers of the U.S. Eximbank.

2. Daniel Bond, *Country Risk Analysis at Ex-Im Bank and the Interagency Country Risk Assessment (ICRAS) Process* (Washington, DC: U.S. Eximbank, 1992), 12–17.

23

Investment Insurance

In addition to export financing assistance, a number of export credit agencies (ECAs) offer insurance covering political risks affecting foreign direct investments. In the 1990s, the major participants in the investment insurance market were twenty-one official ECAs, and the Multilateral Investment Guarantee Agency (MIGA). Most of the official ECAs offering investment insurance were members of the Berne Union (International Union of Export Credit and Investment Insurers). All of these official agencies established their investment insurance programs in the 1960s and 1970s, with the exception of the Overseas Private Investment Corporation (OPIC) in the United States, which was established in 1948, and Instituto per i Servizi Assicurativi e il Credito all' Esportazione (SACE) in Italy, which was set up in 1980. MIGA was set up in 1988 but did not begin active operations until 1990. Although the official programs have been in operation for over ten years, a number of them have very limited activity.

Investment insurance activity of Berne Union members rose substantially from 1985 to 1996, peaking at $15 billion in the latter year. In 1997, however, investment insurance activity fell dramaticaly with the onset of the Asian financial crisis and the resultant setback in foreign direct investment[1] (see Table 23.1). In addition to the official ECAs, investment insurance is offered by a number of private companies. These companies are located in the United States, United Kingdom, France, Sweden, and other countries. There are also a number of Lloyds of London syndicates offering investment insurance. The major underwriting and reinsurance

Table 23.1

Investment Insurance Approval of Berne Union Members (US$ billion)

1985	1986	1987	1988	1989	1990	1991	1992	1993	1994	1995	1996	1997
$2.1	$1.8	$1.3	$2.1	$2.3	$3.2	$4.8	$7.1	$5.8	$12.0	$10.2	$15.0	$9.0

Source: Berne Union.

activity occurs in London. Most of the companies that are not based in London have offices or representatives there. The private underwriters of political risk insurance actively compete with one another but also co-operate to insure joint transactions, with one usually being the lead underwriter that arranges the coverage. This co-operation is necessary to spread risk and create enough capacity to handle the insurance of large projects.

The latest significant entrant to investment insurance, and now its most active offeror, is MIGA, a subsidiary of the World Bank. MIGA will only insure investments in developing countries which are shareholders of MIGA. Among other requirements, MIGA will not conclude any contract of guarantee before the host country has approved the issuance of the guarantee by MIGA. The premium rates charged by MIGA and selected ECAs for investment insurance vary widely as shown in Table 23.2. The factors examined by MIGA and national ECAs prior to approving individual investment insurance applications also show considerable variation, which is shown in Table 23.3.

MIGA requires more information from its clients and does considerably more analysis, than the national ECAs.[2] OPIC, TREUARBEIT, and EFIC are required to look at environmental impact, but others examine this aspect in a cursory way. Among the ECAs, only TREUARBEIT does a legal protection assessment. Virtually no one but MIGA does an economic cost/benefit assessment.

The financial results of overseas investment insurance have been excellent. The two largest official insurers (MIGA and OPIC) have recorded substantial cumulative profits since inception. In fact, at the end of ten years of activity in December 1999, MIGA, the largest insurer of all, had reportedly received only one claim on its entire investment insurance portfolio. Senior officers of MIGA, scarcely believing the results, have joked from time to time about how they hope to receive a few solid claims so that they can pay them promptly and thus underscore the value and importance of the investment insurance product.

Table 23.2
Premium Rates Charged by MIGA and Selected ECAs

Insurer	Premiums/Base Rates		
	Inconvertibility	War	Expropriation
MIGA	0.5%	0.45 - 0.6%	0.6% - 0.25%
	Standby 0.25%	0.2 - 0.25%	0.3 - 0.5%
OPIC	0.3 - 0.5%	0.4 - 0.9%	1.4 - 1.5%
U.S.	Standby 0.253	0.25%	0.25%
EDC	0.3 - 0.5%	0.3 - 0.5%	0.4 - 0.6%
Canada	Standby 0.125%	0.125%	0.125%
EFIC	0.24%	0.24%	0.32%
Australia	Standby 0.12%	0.12%	0.16%
ECGD	0.2 - 0.3%	0.2 - 0.3%	0.3 - 0.4%
U.K.	Standby N/A		
EID/MITI		Combined Premium 0.55% - 1.75%	
Japan			
COFACE	0.4 - 0.6%	0.4 - 0.6%	0.4 - 0.6%
France	Standby N/A		
BFCE		Combined 0.7% - 1.0%	
France			
BEIT		Combined 0.5%, Commitment .0833%	
Germany			

Table 23.3
Factors Examined by MIGA and National ECAs

	Political Risks	Financial Viability	Technical Viability	Economic Costs & Benefits	Legal Protection Assessment	Environment
M IGA	yes	yes	yes	yes	yes	yes
OPIC * (USA)	yes	cursory	cursory	no	no	yes
EDC (Canada)	yes	cursory	cursory	no	no	cursory
EFIC (Australia)	yes	no	no	cursory	no	yes
MITI (Japan)	yes	cursory	cursory	no	no	cursory
TREUARBEIT (Germany)	yes	yes	yes	no	yes	yes

Note: *In addition, OPIC does a "Development Impact Profile, a "U.S. Effects Assessment," and a "Human Rights" Study.

NOTES

1. International Union of Credit and Investment Insurers, *The Berne Union 1999 Yearbook* (London,: Berne Union, 1999), 163.

2. First Washington Associates, *Study of Foreign Direct Investment Trends and Political Risk Investment Insurance Activity* (Arlington, VA: FWA, 1991), 129.

24

The Future for ECAs

A number of trends have recently emerged at export credit agencies (ECAs) that will strongly affect the development of international commerce. For example, the number of ECAs continues to grow rapidly, and their support of national exports is increasing outside the Organization for Economic Cooperation and Development (OECD). The trend toward establishment of new ECAs is expected to continue in the foreseeable future, with much activity in East European, Central Asian, and African countries that do not yet have ECAs. In industrial countries, new private sector ECAs will be established to take advantage of expanding market possibilities.

There is also a strong trend toward growth and consolidation of the largest private ECAs of Western Europe, which are participating in new companies, alliances, joint ventures, and other types of association within Europe and with other parts of the world. The distinctive nature of these ventures is the ability to take advantage of streamlined procedures, economies of scale, and ability to support exports without regard to national content requirements. In Western Europe, a growing amount of trade supported by ECAs has been within and between European Union (EU) members. Exports and imports with Central and Eastern Europe and Central Asia are also growing steadily. There is an increasing interdependence among the ECAs of Western Europe and harmonization of their practices.

In Central and Eastern Europe, countries such as Albania, Croatia, and Bosnia-Herzegovina are studying a variety of ECA options, and although they have not yet established full-service agencies, they will probably do so in the near future. In the former Soviet Union, Kazakstan and Ukraine are converting other types of banks into official ECAs while in Russia the Export and Import Bank may be reoriented to serve as an active trade finance institution.

In Mexico and Canada, ECAs are increasingly supporting regional trade. Political problems in the United States have limited the programs of Export-Import Bank of the United States (Eximbank), but there is growing private sector involvement in export credits, guarantees, and insurance as these become increasingly "domestic" in character in the North American market. In fact, all three countries of North America have private export credit insurers that are expected to increase greatly their share of business underwritten.

In Latin America and the Caribbean, smaller countries of the region are starting to establish official ECAs. This is happening in places such as Costa Rica and Curacao. ECAs in larger countries are being reorganized and improved with new institutions under study or being implemented. This is the case in Argentina, Brazil, and Venezuela. Latin American export trade is becoming increasingly interdependent but remains oriented heavily toward North America and Europe. ECAs in the region are challenged to undertake new programs and policies that will restore dynamism to exports and maximize the private sector contribution.

In Africa, there is a growing movement to establish national ECAs. The larger trading countries, such as South Africa, Egypt, Morocco, Nigeria, and Zimbabwe already have ECAs. Other countries—encouraged by the African Development Bank (AFDB), regional organizations, and bilateral aid agencies—are considering the establishment of new or expanded export credit, guarantee, and insurance organizations. African exports have been essentially stagnant for the last decade, declining as a percentage of world trade, and ECAs are viewed as an important mechanism for reversing this trend.

The ECA situation in Asia reflects the greatest variety of all. This region continues to show substantial growth in exports, due at least partially to official support for export financing. In Japan, it is expected that exporters will continue to make heavy use of export credit insurance as pressures build to increase exports to combat domestic recession. In Korea and Taiwan, reorganizations of ECA responsibilities should be supportive of new growth in exports. The new Export-Import Bank of China should provide increased dynamism to the exports of that country.

In South Asia, India's sophisticated ECA system, particularly its export-import bank, is supporting a growing level of trade. In the Middle East, Turkey's export-import bank is moving aggressively to maximize trade with the former Soviet Union. Jordan established export guarantee and insurance programs in the late 1990s, and other countries in the region are expected to follow suit.

In addition to regional trends in ECA operations, there is a growing move to shorten payment terms on OECD agencies' extensions of export credit and a trend to lengthen payment terms from developing country ECAs. However, it is important to remember that virtually every export credit agency in the world still has a preponderance of short-term credit in its portfolio, reflecting the fact that agricultural goods, raw materials, spare parts, components, and consumer goods, represent a large majority of the items that are traded internationally.

At the regional development banks, significant changes are underway that strongly affect ECAs. The new Export-Import Bank of Africa is moving deliberately to support intra- and extra-regional trade. The Eastern and Southern African Trade and Development Bank (PTA Bank) also offers export finance programs for its members in eastern and central Africa. The Latin American Bank for Exports (BLADEX) remains active throughout Latin America and the Caribbean. The Islamic Development Bank continues its rediscount operations for short-, medium- and long-term exports, and the new Export Credit and Investment Insurance Corporation is increasingly active in the Middle East, Africa, and Asia. The Arab Trade Finance Program restructured its discount programs in the late 1990s and hopes to expand substantially its activity in coming years. The European Bank for Reconstruction and Development offers support for trade finance mechanisms in member countries, but as of 2000, relatively few nations were participants. In the 1990s, the Asian Development Bank approved a $1 billion trade support facility to be administered by the Export-Import Bank of Thailand, but further substantial assistance to ECAs has not yet been forthcoming. The latest multilateral development bank is the Black Sea Trade and Investment Bank, established in 1999, which has announced that trade finance will be one of its major activities.

At the World Bank, several interesting trends are developing. The Latin American and Caribbean divisions have sharply limited support for ECAs, but the divisions handling Central and Eastern Europe, the former Soviet Union, and Africa are providing growing assistance for ECA operations. In Asia, no clear trend has developed, although in late 1999, it was reported that the World Bank was considering substantial new loans to strengthen regional exports, involving several national ECAs.

It is important to note that there is growing pressure to revise export credit payment terms in the OECD arrangement, primarily to accommodate the needs of developing countries for longer repayment periods on major procurement in areas such as municipal infrastructure and environmental development projects. A perceived need to offer longer maturities for projects that are co-financed with the World Bank and others is leading to re-examination of existing term limitations.

As mentioned elsewhere, the use of tied aid or mixed credit by industrial country ECAs has shown a dramatic fall-off in recent years. This is because OECD governments have become increasingly determined to reduce or eliminate subsidies for export credits. Future OECD arrangements are expected to reduce further the use of tied aid.

As a result of new World Trade Organization agreements and rapidly changing trade arrangements, the ECAs of the world have been called upon to support new products in new markets, as well as an increasing volume of traditional exports to familiar destinations. E-commerce and other technological innovations have posed serious operational challenges. The successful marshaling of financial resources and intelligent management of associated risks by the ECAs has done much to determine the course of global economic growth and development in recent years and ECAs' examples of how to finance trade will continue to be widely followed by commercial banks, exporters, and investors.

Appendix A: World's Export Credit, Guarantee, and Insurance Agencies

ARGENTINA	Banco de Inversion y Comercio Exterior (BICE)
	Compañia Argentina de Seguros de Crédito a la Exportacion (CASCE)
AUSTRALIA	Export Finance & Insurance Corporation (EFIC)
	QBE Trade Indemnity Ltd.
AUSTRIA	Oesterreichische Kontrollbank Aktiengesellschaft (OKB)
	Oesterreichische Kreditversicherungs Aktiengesellschaft (OKV)
	Prisma Kreditversicherungs Aktiengesellschaft (PRISMA)
BANGLADESH	Sadharan Bima Corporation Export Credit Guarantee Department (ECGD)
	Central Bank of Bangladesh
BARBADOS	Export Credit Insurance & Guarantee Department of Central Bank
BELGIUM	EULER-COBAC Belguim
	Creditexport
	Institut de Reescompte et de Garantie (IRG)
	Gerling NAMUR
	Office National du Ducroire (OND)
BRAZIL	Banco Nacional de Desenvolvimento Economico e Social (BNDES)
	Export Financing Programme (PROEX)
	Instituto de Reasseguros do Brasil (IRB)
BULGARIA	Bulgarian Export Insurance Agency (BAEZ)

CAMEROON	Fonds d'Aide et de Garantie des Credits aux Petites et Moyennes Enterprises (FOGAPE)
CANADA	Export Development Corporation (EDC)
CHILE	Compania de Seguros de Credito Continental
CHINA	Export-Import Bank of China Peoples Insurance Company of China (PICC)
COLOMBIA	Segurexpo de Colombia, Aseguradora del Comercio Exterior Banco Colombiano de Exportaciones (BANCOLDEX) Fondo Nacional de Garantias (FNG)
COSTA RICA	Fundación Para el Desarrollo Sostenible de la Pequeña y Mediana Empresa (FUNDES)
COTE D'IVOIRE	La Protection Ivoirienne
CROATIA	Croatian Bank for Reconstruction and Development (HBOR)
CUBA	Esicuba
CYPRUS	Export Credit Insurance Service (ECIS)
CZECH REPUBLIC	Ceskoslovenská Obschodni Banka (CSOB) The Export Guarantee & Insurance Corporation (EGAP) Czech Export Bank
DENMARK	EKR Kreditforsikring Eksportkreditfonden (EKF) Danish Export Finance Corporation
ECUADOR	Corporacion Financiera Nacional Fondo de Promoción de Exportaciones (FOPEX)
EGYPT	Export Development Bank of Egypt Export Credit Guarantee Company of Egypt
ESTONIA	Estonian Export Credit State Fund
FINLAND	Finnish Guarantee Board (FGB) Fide Leonia Corporate Bank Pohjola Non-Life Insurance Co. Ltd. (POHJOLA)
FRANCE	Compagnie Francaise d'Assurance pour le Commerce Exterieur (COFACE) Natexis Banque EULER-SFAC Unistrat Assurances
GERMANY	Allgemeine Kreditversicherung Aktiengesellschaft AKA Ausführkredit-Gesellschaft (AKA) C & L Deutsche Revision Aktiengesellschaft Wirtschaftsprufungsgesellschaft (C & L) AKA Gerling Speziale Kreditversicherungs (GERLING) Hermes Kreditversicherungs (HERMES) Kreditanstalt für Wiederaubau (KFW)

GREECE	The Ethniki-Hellenic General Insurance Co. Export Credit Insurance Organization (ECIO)
HONG KONG	Export Credit Insurance Corporation (HKEC)
HUNGARY	Hungarian Export Import Bank (EXIMBANK) Hungarian Export Credit Insurance (MEHIB)
ICELAND	Utflutnings Lanajordur Islands
INDIA	Export Credit Guarantee Corporation of India (ECGC) Export-Import Bank of India (I-EXIMBANK)
INDONESIA	Asuransi Ekspor Indonesia (ASEI)
IRAN	Export Development Bank of Iran (EDBI) Export Guarantee Fund of Iran (EGFI)
IRELAND	Church & General Corporate Insurance (ALLIANZ) Department of Enterprise, Trade and Employment The Insurance Corporation of Ireland (ICI) Clal Credit Insurance Ltd.
ISRAEL	Israel Foreign Trade Risks Insurance Corporation (IFTRIC)
ITALY	Instituto Assicurativi e il Credito all'Esportazione (SACE) EULER-SIAC Societa Italiana Assicurazione Crediti Mediocredito Centrale Societa Italiana Cauzioni (SIC)
JAMAICA	National Export Import Bank of Jamaica (JAMAICA EXIMBANK)
JAPAN	Export Import Bank of Japan (JEXIM) Ministry of Int'l Trade & Industry (EID-MITI)
JORDAN	Jordan Loan Guarantee Corporation (JLGC) Export & Finance Bank (EFB)
KAZAKHSTAN	Export-Import Bank of the Rep. of Kazakhstan (EXIMBANK KAZAKHSTAN)
KENYA	Central Bank of Kenya
LATVIA	JSC Latvian Export Credit (LEC)
LESOTHO	Central Bank of Lesotho
LIBERIA	Liberian Bank of Development and Investment (LBDI)
LITHUANIA	Lietuvas Eksporto ir Importo Draudimas
LUXEMBOURG	Office du Ducroire (ODL)
MALAYSIA	Malaysia Export Credit Insurance (MECIB) Export Import Bank of Malaysia (EXIMBANK) Bank Negara Malaysia
MALTA	Malta Export Credit Insurance (MECI)
MAURITIUS	Development Bank of Mauritius (DBM)

MEXICO	Aseguradora de Creditos y Garantias Banco Mexicano de Comercio Exterior (BANCOMEXT) Compania Mexicana de Seguros de Credito (COMESEC)
NEPAL	Nepal Rastra Bank
NETHERLANDS	Nederlandsche Creditverzekering Maatschappij (NCM)
NEW ZEALAND	EXGO
NIGERIA	Nigerian Export-Import Bank (NEXIM)
NORWAY	Eksportfinans Garanti Instituttet for Eksportkreditt (GIEK) Gerling Nordic Kredittforsikring
OMAN	Export Guarantee and Finance Unit (EGFU)
PAKISTAN	State Bank of Pakistan Pakistan Insurance Corporation
PERU	Corporación Financiera de Desarrollo (COFIDE)
PHILIPPINES	Bangko Sentral Ng Pilipinas (BSP) Philippine Trade and Investment Development Corporation (TIDCORP)
POLAND	Export Credit Insurance Corporation (KUKE) WARTA Insurance & Reinsurance Company Ltd. (WARTA)
PORTUGAL	Companhia de Seguro de Créditos (COSEC)
ROMANIA	Eximbank of Romania
RUSSIAN FEDERATION	Export-Import Bank of the Russian Federation (EXIMBANK OF RUSSIA)
SENEGAL	Agence Senegalaise d'assurance pour le Commerce Exterieur (ASACE)
SINGAPORE	ECICS Credit Insurance Monetary Authority of Singapore (MAS)
SLOVAKIA	Export Credit Insurance Corporation (SPE) Export Import Bank of the Slovak Republic (EXIMBANK)
SLOVENIA	Slovene Export Corporation (SEC)
SOUTH AFRICA	Credit Guarantee Insurance Corporation of Africa (CGIC)
SOUTH KOREA	Export Import Bank of Korea (KEXIMBANK) Korea Export Insurance Corporation (KEIC)
SPAIN	Compañia Española de Seguros de Crédito a la Exportación (CESCE) Compania Espanola de Seguros y Reaseguros de Credito y Caucion (CESCC) Instituto de Credito Oficial (ICO) Mapfre Caucion y Credito Cia. Internacional de Seguros y Reaseguros (MAPFRE)

SRI LANKA	Sri Lanka Export Credit Insurance Corporation (SLECIC)
SWAZILAND	Central Bank of Swaziland Export Credit Guarantee Scheme (ECGS)
SWEDEN	Exportkreditnämnden (EKN) Svensk Export Kredit (SEK)
SWITZERLAND	Federal Eidgenossische Versicherung Aktien Gesellschaft Export Risk Guarantee Agency (ERG)
TAIWAN	The Export-Import Bank of Republic of China (T-EXIMBANK)
THAILAND	Export Import Bank of Thailand
TRINIDAD & TOBAGO	Export Import Bank of Trinidad & Tobago (EXIMBANK)
TURKEY	Export Credit Bank of Turkey (TURK EXIMBANK)
UGANDA	Central Bank of Uganda
UKRAINE	Export-Import Bank of Ukraine
UNITED KINGDOM	Export Credits Guarantee Department (ECGD) EULER Trade Indemnity Plc.
UNITED STATES	Export-Import Bank of the United States (US EXIMBANK) Overseas Private Investment Corporation (OPIC) FCIA Management Company (FCIA) American International Group (AIG) Fidelity & Deposit Co. of Maryland (F&D) Maryland-Netherlands Exporters Insurance Company EULER American Credit Indemnity (ACI) CNA Credit
URUGUAY	Banco de Seguros del Estado Banco Central de Uruguay
UZBEKISTAN	Uzbekinvest National Export Import Insurance Company (UNIC)
VENEZUELA	La Mundial Venezolana de Seguros de Crédito Fondo de Financiamiento a las Exportaciones (FINEXPO) Export Import Bank of Venezuela
ZAMBIA	Zambia Export and Import Bank (ZEXIM)
ZIMBABWE	Credit Insurance Zimbabwe (CREDSURE) Reserve Bank of Zimbabwe (RBZ)

MULTILATERAL EXPORT CREDIT AGENCIES

African Export-Import Bank (AFREXIMBANK)

Arab Trade Finance Program (ATFP)

Banco Latino-Americano de Exportaciones (BLADEX)

Black Sea Trade and Development Bank
Central American Bank for Economic Integration (CABEI)
Corporacion Andina de Fomento (CAF)
Inter Arab Investment Guarantee Corporation (IAIGC)
Islamic Corporation for the Insurance of Investment & Export Credit (ICIEC)
Islamic Development Bank (IsDB)
Inter-American Development Bank (IADB)
Multilateral Investment Guarantee Agency (MIGA)
Organization of Eastern Caribbean States (OECS)
PTA Bank

Appendix B: Arrangement on Guidelines for Officially Supported Export Credits

CHAPTER I: SCOPE OF THE ARRANGEMENT

1. Participation

a. The Participants to the Arrangement are: Australia, Canada, the European Community (which includes the following countries: Austria, Belgium, Denmark, Finland, France, Germany, Greece, Ireland, Italy, Luxembourg, the Netherlands, Portugal, Spain, Sweden, and the United Kingdom) Japan, Korea, New Zealand, Norway, Switzerland and the United States.

b. The Participants agree to respect and to apply the terms of the Arrangement. Other countries willing to apply these Guidelines may become Participants following prior invitation of the existing Participants.

2. Scope of Application

The Arrangement shall apply to all official support for exports of goods and/or services, or to financial leases, which have repayment terms (as defined in Article 8) of two years or more. This is regardless of whether the official support for export credits is given by means of direct credits/financing, refinancing, interest rate support, guarantee or insurance. The Arrangement shall also apply to official support in the form of tied aid.

3. Special Sectoral Applications and Exclusions

The Participants shall apply special guidelines to the following sectors:
a. *Ships*

The Arrangement shall apply to ships not covered by the Understanding on Export Credits for Ships (Annex I). Where a Participant intends to support terms for a ship covered by the Understanding—and therefore not by this Arrangement—that would be more favourable than those terms permitted by this Arrangement, the Participant shall notify all other Participants of such terms. The appropriate procedures for notification are set out in Article 49.

b. *Nuclear Power Plant*

The Arrangement shall apply, except that where a corresponding provision exists in the Sector Understanding on Export Credits for Nuclear Power Plant (Annex II), which complements the Arrangement, the Sector Understanding shall prevail. The Arrangement shall apply to official support provided for the decommissioning of nuclear power plant, i.e. the closing down or dismantling of nuclear power plant.

c. *Aircraft*

The Arrangement shall apply, except that where a corresponding provision exists in the Sector Understanding on Export Credits for Civil Aircraft (Annex III), which complements the Arrangement, the Sector Understanding shall prevail.

d. *Exclusions*

The Arrangement does not apply to official support relating to exports of:

—Military Equipment; or

—Agricultural Commodities.

4. Review

The Participants shall review, at least annually, the functioning of the Arrangement. Its provisions can be revised by review as set out in Articles 82, 83 and 84.

5. Withdrawal

The Arrangement is of indefinite duration, nevertheless a Participant may withdraw by notifying the other Participants in writing by means of instant communication, e.g., the OECD On-line Information System (OLIS), telex, telefax. The withdrawal takes effect 60 calendar days after receipt of the notification by the Participants.

6. Monitoring

The Secretariat shall monitor the implementation of the Arrangement.

CHAPTER II: PROVISIONS FOR EXPORT CREDITS

7. Cash Payments

a. The Participants shall require purchasers of goods and services which are the subject of official support to make cash payments of a minimum of 15 per cent of the export contract value at or before the starting point of credit as defined in Article 9.

b. The export contract value is the total amount to be paid by or on behalf of the purchaser for goods and/or services exported, i.e. excluding local costs as defined in Article 25 and also interest. In the case of a lease, it excludes the portion of the lease payment that is equivalent to interest.

c. Official support for such cash payments can only take the form of insurance and guarantees, i.e., pure cover, against the usual pre-credit risks.

d. For the assessment of cash payments, the export contract value may be reduced proportionally if the transaction includes goods and services from a third country which are not officially supported.

e. Retention payments made after the starting point of credit are not regarded as cash payments in this context.

8. Repayment Terms

The repayment term is the period beginning at the starting point of credit, as defined in Article 9, and ending on the contractual date of the final payment.

9. Starting Point of Credit

The definition in the Arrangement is based on the Berne Union definition of the term "starting point of credit":

a. In the case of a contract for the sale of capital goods consisting of individual items useable in themselves (e.g. locomotives), the starting point is the mean date or actual date when the buyer takes physical possession of the goods in his own country.

b. In the case of a contract for the sale of capital equipment for complete plant or factories where the supplier has no responsibility for commissioning, the starting point is the date at which the buyer is to take physical possession of the entire equipment (excluding spare parts) supplied under the contract.

c. In the case of construction contracts where the contractor has no responsibility for commissioning, the starting point is the date when construction has been completed.

d. In the case of any contract where the supplier or contractor has a contractual responsibility for commissioning the plant, the starting point is the date when, after installation or construction, preliminary tests to ensure that it is ready for operation have been completed. This applies whether or not it is handed over to the buyer at that time in accordance with the terms of the contract and irrespective of any continuing commitment which the supplier or contractor may have (e.g. for guaranteeing its effective functioning or training local personnel).

e. In the cases of the sub-paragraphs b.–d. above, where the contract involves the separate execution of individual parts of a project, the date of the starting point for each separate part, or the mean date of those starting points, or, where the supplier has a contract, not for the whole project but for an essential part of it, the starting point may be that appropriate to the project as a whole.

10. Maximum Repayment Term

The maximum repayment term varies according to the classification of the country of destination determined by the criteria in Article 12.

a. For Category I countries, the maximum repayment term is five years, with the possibility of agreeing eight-and-a-half years when the procedures for prior notification set out in Article 49 are followed.

b. For Category II countries, the maximum repayment term is 10 years.

c. Official support shall not be provided if there is clear evidence that the contract has been structured with a purchaser in a country which is not the final destination of the goods exclusively with the aim of obtaining more favourable repayment terms.

d. In the event of a contract involving more than one country of destination the Participants should seek to establish a common line in accordance with the procedures in Articles 71 to 77 to reach agreement on appropriate terms.

11. Special Terms for Power Plant Other Than Nuclear Power Plant

a. For power plant other than nuclear power plant, the maximum repayment term shall be twelve years. If a Participant intends to support a repayment term longer than five years for Category I countries or a repayment term longer than 10 years for Category II countries, the Participant shall give prior notification in accordance with the procedure in Article 49.

b. Power plant other than nuclear power plant are complete power stations, or parts thereof, not fuelled by nuclear power; they include all components, equipment, materials, and services (including the training of personnel) directly required for the construction and commissioning of such non-nuclear power stations. This does not include items for which the buyer is usually responsible, e.g., costs associated with land development, roads, construction villages, power lines, and switchyard and water supply; as well as costs arising from official approval procedures (e.g., site permits, construction permits, fuel loading permits) in the buyer's country.

12. Classification of Countries for Maximum Repayment Terms

a. Category I countries are those which are on the World Bank's graduation list.[1] All other countries are in Category II. The World Bank graduation level is recalculated on an annual basis. A country will change category only after its World Bank category has remained unchanged for two consecutive years.

b. The following operational criteria and procedures apply when classifying countries.

1. Classification for Arrangement purposes is determined by per capita GNP as calculated by the World Bank for the purposes of the World Bank classification of borrowing countries.

2. In cases where the World Bank does not have enough information to publish per capita GNP data, the World Bank shall be asked to estimate whether the

country in question has a per capita GNP above or below the current threshold. The country shall be classified according to the estimate unless the Participants decide to act otherwise.

3. If a country is reclassified in accordance with Article 12 a) the reclassification will take effect two weeks after the conclusions drawn from the above-mentioned data from the World Bank have been communicated to all Participants by the Secretariat.

4. In cases where the World Bank revises figures, such revisions shall be disregarded in relation to the Arrangement. Nevertheless, the classification of a country may be changed by way of a common line and Participants would favourably consider a change due to errors and omissions in the figures subsequently recognised in the same calendar year in which the figures were first distributed by the Secretariat.

13. Repayment of Principal

a. The principal sum of an export credit shall normally be repaid in equal and regular instalments not less frequently than every six months, with the first instalment to be made no later than six months after the starting point of credit.

b. In the case of leases, this profile of repayments may be applied either for the amount of principal only, or for the amount of principal and interest combined.

c. Prior notification according to Article 49 is required if a Participant does not intend to follow this practice.

14. Payment of Interest

a. Interest shall not normally be capitalised during the repayment period, but shall be payable not less frequently than every six months, with the first payment to be made no later than six months after the starting point of credit.

b. Prior notification in accordance with Article 49 is required if a Participant does not intend to follow this practice.

c. Interest excludes:

—any payment by way of premium or other charge for insuring or guaranteeing supplier credits or financial credits. Where official support is provided by means of direct credits/financing or refinancing, the premium either may be added to the face value of the interest rate or may be a separate charge; both components are to be specified separately to the Participants;

—any other payment by way of banking fees or commissions relating to the export credit other than annual or semi-annual bank charges that are payable throughout the repayment period; and

—withholding taxes imposed by the importing country.

15. Minimum Interest Rates

The Participants providing official financing support through direct credits/ financing, refinancing, or interest rate support shall apply minimum interest rates; the Participants shall apply the relevant Commercial Interest Reference Rates (CIRRs). CIRRs are interest rates established according to the following principles:

— CIRRs should represent final commercial lending interest rates in the domestic market of the currency concerned;

— CIRRs should closely correspond to the rate for first-class domestic borrowers;

— CIRRs should be based, where appropriate, on the funding cost of fixed interest-rate finance over a period of no less than five years;

— CIRRs should not distort domestic competitive conditions; and

— CIRRs should closely correspond to a rate available to first-class foreign borrowers.

16. Construction of CIRRs

a. With the principles in Article 15 in mind, CIRRs shall be set at a fixed margin of 100 basis points above their respective base rates unless Participants have agreed otherwise.

b. Each Participant shall initially select one of the following two base rate systems for its national currency:

— three-year government bond yields for repayment terms of up to and including five-years; five-year government bond yields for over five and up to and including eight and a half years; and seven-year government bond yields for over eight-and-a-half years; or

— five-year government bond yields for all maturities.

Exceptions to the base rate system shall be agreed by the Participants.

c. The exceptions to the base rate system are the Yen CIRR, which is based on the LTPR (Long-term prime rate) minus 20 basis points for all maturities; and the ECU CIRR, which is based on the secondary market yield on medium term ECU bonds in the Luxembourg stock exchange plus 50 basis points.

d. Other Participants shall use this selection should they decide to finance in that currency.

e. A Participant may change its base rate system after giving six months' advance notice and with the counsel of the Participants.

f. A Participant which wishes to provide official support in the currency of a country which is not a Participant may make a proposal for the construction of the CIRR in that currency using common line procedures in accordance with Articles 70 to 77.

17. Application of CIRRs

a. The interest rate applying to a transaction shall not be fixed for a period longer than 120 days. A margin of 20 basis points shall be added to the CIRR if the terms of the official financing support are fixed before the contract date.

b. Where official financing support is provided for floating rate loans, banks and other financing institutions shall not be allowed to offer the option of the lower of either the CIRR (at time of the original contract) or the short-term market rate throughout the life of the loan.

18. Cosmetic Interest Rates

Cosmetic interest rates are rates below the relevant CIRR which benefit from official support, and which may involve a compensatory measure including a corresponding increase in the contract value or other contractual adjustment.

19. Official Support for Cosmetic Interest Rates

a. Official financing support by means of direct financing shall not be provided at rates below the relevant CIRR.
b. Official support may be provided by the following means:

—official financing support, other than specified above, as long as such support is not offered at cosmetic interest rates; and/or

—official support in the form of insurance and guarantees, i.e. pure cover.

c. If there is an enquiry from another Participant about a transaction, the Participant which intends to support the transaction should use its best endeavours to clarify the financial terms and mechanisms, including the compensatory measure.

d. A Participant with information which suggests that non-conforming terms may have been offered by another Participant shall make reasonable efforts to determine whether or not the transaction benefits from official financing support, and whether or not the terms of this support conform to the provisions of Article 15 of the Arrangement. This Participant will be considered to have made such reasonable efforts if it has informed, by means of instant communication, the other Participant assumed to have offered such non-conforming terms, of its intention to match. Unless the Participant allegedly offering the non-conforming terms declares within three working days that the transaction does not benefit from official financing support or that the terms of the official financing support conform to the provisions of Article 15 of the Arrangement, the matching Participant has the right to match these terms according to the procedure in Article 50.

20. Minimum Premium

a. The Participants providing official support through direct credits/financing, refinancing, export credit insurance and guarantees, shall charge no less than the minimum premium benchmarks for the sovereign credit risk and the country credit risk, irrespective of whether the buyer/borrower is a private or public entity.

b. Sovereign credit risk is the full faith and credit of the State, e.g. the Ministry of Finance or the Central Bank.

c. Country credit risk is the assessment of whether a country will service its external debts. The five elements of country credit risk are:

—general moratorium on repayments decreed by the buyer's/borrower's/guarantor's government or by that agency of a country through which repayment is effected;

—political events and/or economic difficulties arising outside the country of the notifying Participant or legislative/administrative measures taken outside the country of the notifying Participant which prevent or delay the transfer of funds paid over in respect of the credit;

—legal provisions adopted in the buyer's/borrower's country declaring repayments made in local currency to be a valid discharge of the debt, notwithstanding that, as a result of fluctuations in exchange rates, such repayments, when converted into the currency of the credit, no longer cover the amount of the debt at the date of the transfer of funds;

—any other measure or decision of the government of a foreign country which prevents repayment under a credit; and

—cases of force majeure occurring outside the country of the notifying Participant, i.e. war (including civil war), expropriation, revolution, riot, civil disturbances, cyclones, floods, earthquakes, eruptions, tidal waves and nuclear accidents.

d. The minimum premium benchmarks shall be established in accordance with the principles set out in Articles 21 to 23.

e. The Participants may charge at a level above the minimum premium benchmarks.

21. Country Risk Classification Methodology

a. Premium shall be risk based.

b. To assess the risk and to establish a common reference classification of countries, they are scored according to the Quantitative Country Risk Model (the Model):

—the Model is based, for each country, on three groups of risk indicators: the payment experience of the Participants, the financial situation and the economic situation;

—the methodology of the Model consists of different steps including the assessment of the three groups of risk indicators, and the combination and flexible weighting of the risk indicator groups; and

—such scoring results in countries being classified into seven risk categories.

c. In accordance with procedures agreed by the Participants, the quantitative outcome of the Model shall be considered country-by-country to integrate, in a qualitative way, the political risk and/or other risk factors not taken into account by the Model; if appropriate, this may lead to an adjustment to the Model classification to reflect the final assessment of the country credit risk.

22. Minimum Premium Benchmarks[2]

a. Premium shall converge. To ensure convergence, minimum premium benchmarks, consistent with the level of risk, not inadequate to cover long term operating costs and losses and taking into account a set of standard related conditions, shall be determined as follows:

—minimum premium benchmarks are established for each of the seven risk categories;

—the standard product to which the minimum premium benchmarks relate shall be insurance with 95 percent cover, proportionately adjusted for the amount at risk, with cover of interest during the claims waiting period of six months without a separate premium surcharge; and

—direct credits/financing shall be considered as standard products for 100 percent cover.

b. the "High Income OECD countries" (as defined by the World Bank)[3] as well as other countries with similar risks shall not be subject to the application of minimum premium benchmarks with the understanding that the pricing of the private market shall not be undercut.

c. The "highest risk" countries in Category seven shall, in principle, be subject to appropriate premium surcharges to the minimum premium benchmarks established for that Category; any such surcharges shall be set by the Participant providing official support.

d. There shall be differentiated minimum premium benchmarks for sovereign credit risk and country credit risk.

e. The minimum premium benchmarks for sovereign credit risk shall be the minimum rates for public sector risk and private sector risk where both the country risk and the buyer/borrower risk are covered.

f. In situations where the buyer/borrower risk is excluded, the minimum country credit risk premium benchmark shall be set at 90 percent of the minimum sovereign credit risk premium benchmark, i.e., a discount of 10 percent from the minimum sovereign credit risk premium benchmark may be applied.

g. Minimum premium benchmarks are expressed in percentages of the principal value of the credit as if premium were collected in full at the date of the credit, insurance or guarantee as illustrated in the Electronic Exchange of Information (EEI) referred to in Annex VII.

23. Related Conditions

a. To accommodate the differing quality of products provided by the Participants, the minimum premium benchmarks shall be adjusted to take account of the related conditions. The treatment of related conditions shall be based on the exporter's perspective (i.e., to neutralise the competitive effect arising from the differing qualities of product provided to the exporter/financial institution), and three related conditions:

—the percentage of cover;

—the claims waiting period, i.e., the period between the due date of payment by the buyer/borrower and the date that the insurer/guarantor is liable to reimburse the exporter/financial institution; and

—the cover of interest during the claims waiting period without surcharge.

b. to take account of non-standard related conditions, the minimum premium benchmarks are adjusted upwards or downwards. All existing products of the Participants shall be classified into one of the three product categories which are:

—below standard product, i.e., insurance without cover of interest during the claims waiting period and insurance with cover of interest during the claims waiting period with an appropriate premium surcharge;

—standard product, i.e., insurance with cover of interest during the claims waiting period without an appropriate premium surcharge and direct credits/financing; and

—above standard product, i.e., unconditional guarantees.

c. Pricing differentials shall reflect the quality differences of all three product categories; these pricing differentials shall attribute surcharges in the case of above standard products and premium discounts in the case of below standard products.

d. Minimum premium benchmarks shall be adjusted for each percentage of cover, above and below the standard percentage of cover, i.e., 95 percent.

24. Premium Feedback Tools

a. Premium shall not be inadequate to cover long term operating costs and losses. To ensure the adequacy of premium benchmarks and to allow, if necessary, for adjustments, either upwards or downwards:

—three premium feedback tools (PFTs), shall be used in parallel to monitor and adjust the minimum premium benchmarks; and

—the PFTs are the accruals and cashflow accounting approaches collated on an aggregate Participants' level and, where appropriate, private market indicators.

b. It is understood that:

—the use of the PFTs shall not require the Participants to change their existing accounting systems and practices;

—all officially supported export credits which take the form of direct credits/financing, refinancing, export credit insurance or guarantees to which the Arrangement applies shall be reported;

—only sovereign and country credit risk shall be reported, irrespective of whether the buyer risk is covered;

—the PFTs shall use a common start date; and

—the concept of claims shall encompass refinanced debts under direct credits/financing, refinancing, export credit insurance or guarantees; it shall also encompass rolled-over, overdue and defaulted loans.

25. Local Costs

a. Local Costs consist of expenditure for goods and services in the buyer's country, that are necessary either for executing the exporter's contract or for completing the project of which the exporter's contract forms a part. These exclude commission payable to the exporter's agent in the buying country.

b. Official Support shall not be provided for more than 100 percent of the value of the goods and services exported, including those supplied by third countries, but excluding local costs. In consequence, the amount of local costs supported on credit terms shall not exceed the amount of the cash payment. Official support for local costs shall not be provided on more favourable terms than agreed for the related exports.

c. For Category I countries official support for local costs shall be confined to insurance and guarantees, i.e., pure cover, and shall not involve official financing support.

26. Validity Period for Export Credits

Credit terms and conditions for an individual export credit or line of credit shall not be fixed for a period exceeding six months. A line of credit is a framework, in whatever form, for export credits that covers a series of transactions which may or may not be linked to a specific project.

27. No Derogation Engagement for Export Credits

a. The Participants shall not derogate from maximum repayment terms, minimum interest rates, minimum premium benchmarks (after adjustment for related conditions), the six-month limitation on the validity period for export credit terms and conditions, or extend the repayment term by extending the repayment date of the first instalment of principal set out in Article 13a).

b. Notwithstanding sub paragraph a. above, a Participant may, subject to the procedures set out in Article 48, apply a premium benchmark below the minimum benchmark (after adjustment for related conditions) when the country credit risk (as detailed in Article 20) is either externalised/removed or limited/excluded for the entire life of the debt repayment obligation, as follows:

—if a Participant is able to externalise/remove the five elements of country credit risk (for the entire life of the debt repayment obligation) as detailed in Article 20, the minimum premium benchmark shall be determined by the country credit risk of the jurisdiction to which the risk has been transferred.

—if a Participant is able to limit/exclude any of the five elements of country credit risk (for the entire life of the debt repayment obligation), the Participant may apply an appropriate discount to the minimum premium benchmark. The expectation is that any discount where the transfer risk, as set out in the first and second tiret of Article 20 c. is excluded, should not exceed 50 percent of the minimum premium benchmark.

—each Permitted Exception to the minimum premium benchmarks shall be on a case by case basis and shall not be taken as a precedent for any future case by any Participant.

28. Action to Avoid or Minimise Losses

The Arrangement does not prevent export credit insurance authorities or financing institutions from agreeing more favourable terms and conditions than permitted if such action is taken after the contract award (when the export credit agreement and ancillary documents have already become effective) and where the intention is solely to avoid or minimise loss from events which could give rise to non-payment or claims.

29. Matching

a. The Participants may match credit terms and conditions notified according to the procedures in Articles 47, 48 and 49, as well as credit terms and conditions not notified or those supported by non-Participants. The matching support may not extend beyond the validity period of the credit terms and conditions being matched.

b. The Participants shall match credit terms and conditions by supporting terms that comply with the Arrangement, unless the initiating offer itself does not comply with the Arrangement. Where matching involves minimum premium benchmarks, the Participants shall be free to match the rate only if it is providing support on the basis of a similar quality risk, also taking into account product quality. A Participant intending to match credit terms and conditions:

—notified by another Participant shall follow the procedures in Articles 50 or 51 as appropriate;

—not notified by a Participant shall follow the procedures in Article 52; or

—supported by a non-Participant shall follow the procedures in Article 53.

NOTES

1. For example using 1996 data, those countries with a GNP per capita above $5,435.

2. The application of the minimum premium benchmarks is subject to the Transition Period:

—The Transition Period shall end on 31st March 1999 following which the Guiding Principles shall be immediately implemented.

—Premium rates which have been fixed during the Transition Period shall not be valid beyond three months from 31st March 1999, i.e. 30th June 1999.

—During the Transition Period, there shall be best endeavours not to reduce premium rates below the initial minimum premium benchmarks, except in the case of matching.

—Korea

* The Transition Period for Korea shall end on 31st March 2002.

* By 1st April 1999, Korea shall apply at least 40 per cent of the initial minimum premium benchmarks; by 1st April 2000, Korea shall apply 60 per cent of the minimum premium benchmarks; by 1st April 2001, Korea shall apply 80 per cent of the minimum premium benchmarks; and by 1st April 2002, Korea shall apply 100 per cent of the benchmarks.

3. For example using 1996 data, those countries with a GNP per capita above $9,635.

Appendix C: Fact Sheet— Proposed OECD Premium Agreement

MAY 9, 1997

Application

The minimum premium (exposure fee) benchmark rates:

- will apply to all official export credit transactions with a repayment term of two years or more, with the exception of large commercial aircraft, agricultural products, and ships;
- are established for each total term length (repayment period + ½ disbursement period) within each of seven country categories; and
- notwithstanding exceptional circumstances (see below) represent a "floor" for each market, regardless of the type of risk (i.e., sovereign, public, or private).

Timing/Transition Issues

- For all countries, there will be a two-year transition period before any provisions of the agreement are applicable (effective date of 4/1/99).
- Korea must change rates which are no less than 40 percent of the minimum benchmarks by 4/1/99, and must be in complete compliance by 4/1/02.

During the transition period:

- no ECA shall lower its premium rate (exposure fee) schedule;
- an on-line information system with each country's premium rates (among other things) will operate to provide transparency; and
- a definitive list of "permitted exceptions" (i.e., rare and unusual situations where below-benchmark rates may be applied—with *prior notification*) will be finalized.

After the transition period:

- all countries must abide by the minimum premium benchmarks applicable to their program; and
- ECA will have the right to match a lower rate provided by any competitor (including Korea) and for any reason.

Validity/Recalibration of Benchmark Rate Schedule

- The initial benchmarks shall last for at least one year.
- After one year, the overall level of the benchmark rates and all other aspects of the agreement shall be reviewed at least once a year in the context of three separate financial performance measurements; according to a cash flow analysis and an accruals accounting tool, and against private market measures of risk (i.e., sovereign bond yields).
- The reclassification of markets will occur at least annually.

Table C.1
Proposed Benchmarks: May 5, 1997

% Cover	"Quality" of Product	Country Risk Category						
		1	2	3	4	5	6	7
100 %	above standard	1.58	3.13	5.27	7.87	10.85	13.79	16.77
	standard	1.58	3.11	5.19	7.74	10.66	13.52	16.44
	below standard	1.57	3.08	5.12	7.60	10.47	13.25	15.78
97.5 %	above standard	1.54	3.04	5.13	7.61	10.39	13.08	15.87
	standard	1.54	3.02	5.05	7.48	10.22	12.82	15.56
	below standard	1.53	3.00	4.98	7.35	10.04	12.57	14.94
95 %	above standard	1.51	2.96	4.98	7.36	9.94	12.37	14.97
	standard	1.50	2.94	4.91	7.23	9.77	12.13	14.68
	below standard	1.49	2.92	4.84	7.10	9.60	11.89	14.09
90 %	above standard	1.43	2.80	4.72	6.97	9.42	11.72	14.19
	standard	1.42	2.79	4.65	6.85	9.26	11.49	13.91
	below standard	1.42	2.77	4.58	6.73	9.09	11.26	13.35

Appendix D:
Glossary of Technical Terms

Acts of God: *See* **Force Majeure**.

Advance Payment Bond: Bond issued by a financial institution to a foreign buyer, ensuring the buyer that it can recover the amount of its advance payment to the exporter if it is dissatisfied with the goods or services delivered by the exporter.

Adverse Selection: The concept of an exporter seeking to insure only more risky buyers or countries, rather than all buyers in all countries, for short-term export credit insurance. Export credit agencies seek to avoid adverse selection either by requiring whole turnover or by charging higher premiums and/or limiting the percentage of coverage granted for risky transactions. *See* **Reasonable Spread of Risk** and **Specific Coverage**.

A Forfait: The purchase, without recourse to the exporter, of medium-term negotiable instruments guaranteed by a bank, arising from the export of goods or services. All risks are thereby passed on to the purchaser of the claim (the forfaiter) who pays the seller cash after deducting an interest charge (discount).

Bankers' Acceptance: A negotiable draft, normally arising from a time letter of credit drawn on a bank which the bank has agreed by its acceptance to pay at a specified date in the future. Banker's acceptances usually finance short-term, self-liquidating transactions including both exports and imports. When accepted by a prime bank, the bankers' acceptance becomes a marketable instrument that can be sold at a discount as an attractive short-term instrument for investors.

Berne Union: The International Union of Credit and Investment Insurers, commonly known as the "Berne Union," provides for the free exchange of ideas and information through "international acceptance of sound principles of export credit insurance, and the establishment and maintenance of discipline in the terms of international trade." Established in Berne, Switzerland, in 1934, the Berne Union now has its headquarters in London and has over forty members from developing and industrial countries.

Bid Bond: Bond issued by a financial institution on behalf of a supplier when bidding on a major project. It normally covers about 5 percent of the bid contract price. A bid bond will compensate the buyer if the supplier fails to fulfill the terms of the bid after having been declared the successful bidder. In some countries, insurance or guarantee coverage is available to protect the supplier and financial institution issuing the bond from the unjustified or capricious calling of the bid bond.

Buyer Credit: Financial arrangement in which a bank and/or an export credit agency makes a loan directly to the overseas purchaser. Generally the proceeds can be used only to purchase specific imports. Disbursements may be made either directly to the exporter or to reimburse the buyer for payments already made to the exporter. Contrasts with **Supplier Credit**.

Capital: The funds provided by the sponsors (owners) of an export credit agency plus the accumulated gains or losses from operations and investments, less specific reserves set aside for claims and extraordinary losses. *See* **Reserves**.

Case Reserves: Reserves set aside by an export credit agency to meet anticipated payments to exporters based on claims or notices of problems filed by exporters for specific transactions. Case reserves relate to specific transactions as contrasted with general reserves. *See* **Reserves**.

Cash Payment: The portion of the contract price related to medium- and long-term credits that the foreign buyer must pay the exporter on or before delivery of the goods or services. The minimum cash payment is generally 15 percent of the contract price.

Catastrophic Risks: Risks resulting from natural disasters in the foreign buyer's country, such as earthquakes, floods, etc., which prevents the foreign buyer from making payment when due. *See* **Force Majeure**.

Category I, II, and III Countries: Under the OECD arrangement, Category I countries are those with 1979 per capita income of $4,000 p.a. and higher, Category II countries are those not classified as I or III, and Category III countries are those eligible for International Development Agency (IDA) credits and others where per capita GNP does not exceed IDA eligibility levels.

Claim: An application filed with an export credit agency for payment under an export credit insurance policy or guarantee to an insured/guaranteed bank or exporter resulting from nonpayment by a foreign buyer.

Coinsurance: Export credit risk assumed jointly by two or more export credit insurers on an export transaction.

Commercial Interest Reference Rates (CIRRs): Minimum interest rates that may be supported by ECAs adhering to the OECD arrangement. CIRRs are based upon government bond yields plus 100 basis points.

Commercial Risk: Risk of nonpayment on an export credit by a buyer or borrower in the event of bankruptcy, insolvency, protracted default, and/or failure to take up goods that have been shipped according to the supply contract. Export credit agencies will generally not cover commercial risks on sales to affiliated firms and nonpayment arising from disputes between the parties to the export contract about product quality, supplier performance, and so forth.

Commitment Fee: The fee charged by a lender to compensate for having committed funds, based on undisbursed balances. Many export credit agencies charge commitment fees.

Comprehensive Coverage: Insurance or guarantee cover that combines both commercial risk coverage and political risk coverage.

Concessionality Level: The total value of subsidy provided in connection with export financing. For example, a grant could be considered to have a concessionality level of 100%. If a grant covered 25% of an export's value and traditional export credit covered the balance of export value, the concessionality level would be 25%.

Consensus: Commonly called the Organization for Economic Cooperation and Development (OECD) Consensus or Arrangement on Export Credits, it is an agreement concluded in February 1976 among major industrial countries that established guidelines for maximum repayment terms and minimum interest rates, and procedures for the notification of nonadherence to these guidelines. The consensus was superseded in April 1978 by the Arrangement on Guidelines for Officially Supported Export Credits and accepted by twenty members of the OECD Export Credit Group *See* **OECD Arrangement**.

Consignment Insurance: Export credit insurance on goods held for resale outside the country where the goods were produced. Consignment insurance covers noncommercial risks such as requisition, expropriation, or the imposition of any law, decree, or regulation that prevents the re-export of these goods.

Conversion Risk: Risk that, after a foreign buyer makes the required payment in the local currency, the payment cannot be converted to the currency required by the sales contract and transferred to the country of the exporter. Conversion risk is usually covered under political risk insurance. Also called **Transfer Risk**.

Cost-Escalation Insurance: *See* **Inflation Insurance**.

Country Categories: Classification of buyer countries, usually in four or five classes, according to varying degrees of political risks perceived. Letter ratings, e.g., *A* for low risk countries to *D* or *E* for high risk, are often used. Premium rates generally vary by country category.

Country Exposure: *See* **Exposure**.

Deductible: The amount of loss under commercial risk insurance that is incurred by the insured for its own account for each policy period. *See* **First Loss**.

Default: Failure of a buyer or guarantor (if any) to pay either principal or interest when due, provided the goods have been delivered and accepted.

Delegated Authority: The authority granted by an export credit agency to a commercial bank or exporter to commit insurance or guarantees for specified amounts and under certain conditions without prior specific approval. It is usually granted to banks or exporters based on prior experience and demonstrated capacity to comply with program requirements.

Direct Loan: Loan from an export financing agency to a foreign buyer for the purchase of specific goods or services on credit terms. The loan usually is secured by a bank guarantee in the buyer's country or by an export credit insurance policy.

Discount Loan: A commercial bank loan to an exporter made at a discount from the amount of a related export receivable. A bank loan to a foreign buyer may also be discounted by a government export finance institution.

Discretionary Credit Limit (DCL): The maximum amount of credit per buyer on which an insured exporter may ship and receive insurance coverage under an export credit insurance policy without prior approval of the specific buyer by the export credit insurance agency.

Exchange Risk Insurance: Insurance coverage that protects the exporter from a negative variation in the exchange rate on foreign-currency denominated contracts or credits. An export credit agency generally will insure exchange risks only for periods longer than one year.

Eximbank: Export credit agency offering a full range of financial programs, with the organizational and legal structure of a bank.

Export Credit: Pre-shipment or post-shipment financing extended by a commercial bank or export credit agency to an exporter or foreign buyer.

Export Credit Agency (ECA): A financial agency directed to offering loans, guarantees, credit insurance, or financial technical assistance to support exports.

Export Credit Insurance: Insurance covering exporters against nonpayment by their foreign customers.

Exporter Participation: The portion of the risk of nonpayment on a post-shipment credit to a foreign buyer retained by an exporter. Also called *exporter retention. See* **Retention**.

Exporter Retention: *See* **Exporter Participation**.

Exporter Risk: The risk that a foreign buyer will refuse to pay an export credit because of the failure of the exporter to fulfill the terms of the export contract.

Exposure: Amount for which an export credit agency, commercial bank, or exporter may be liable in the event of nonpayment by a given foreign buyer or by all buyers in a given country.

Factoring: The sale of short-term export receivables, usually without recourse to the exporter.

Filing Period: The time period within which a claim must be filed with the export credit insurance agency if the claim is to be valid. The filing period typically extends from six to nine months after the waiting period.

Financial Credit: Loan to a foreign financial institution by an official export credit agency, used by the foreign institution for financing individual export transactions.

Financial Guarantee: A commitment or assurance that in the event of nonpayment of an export credit by a foreign borrower, the export credit agency will indemnify the financing bank if the terms and conditions of its guarantees are fulfilled. These guarantees often cover 100 percent of the outstanding principal and a specified amount of interest.

First Loss: An amount normally borne by the insured, which is absorbed before any claim payment is calculated under the export credit insurance policy. Also called a **Deductible**.

Force Majeure: Events over which none of the parties to an export transaction has control or influence. Also known as *Acts of God*. *See* **Catastrophic Risk**.

Foreign Content: Any portion or value added to an exported good or service that is manufactured, assembled, or supplied from another country. An export credit agency may restrict its support of foreign content to a percentage of the total contract or in proportion to the domestic content of the contract.

Forfaiting: *See* **A Forfait**.

Global Policy: An export credit insurance policy that covers the short-term credits extended to all of an exporter's foreign buyers during a specified time period. Depending on the export credit agency's policies, a global policy can be comprehensive or cover only political or only commercial risks.

Grace Period: An interval of time allowed to the borrower by the lender after loan proceeds are disbursed and before repayment of principal begins.

Guarantee: Used generally to denote any assurance of payment or compensation given to the entity financing an export credit, which is to be honored in the event of default or nonpayment by the primary obligor.

Guarantor: An individual, company, financial institution, or government entity that guarantees payment of an export credit.

Guardian Authority: The parent or superior entity of an export credit agency, such as the Central Bank or Ministry of Finance, sometimes also the principal shareholder, which provides guidance to and may offer an implied or contractual guarantee of the obligations of the export credit agency.

High Credit Outstanding: The largest amount owed by a foreign buyer to an exporter or commercial bank at a point in time, represented by one or more transactions. It also can refer to the maximum exposure of an export credit insurance agency to a single foreign buyer. *See* **Exposure**.

Hold Harmless Agreement: A special form of guarantee by an export credit insurer that assures payment to the financing commercial bank irrespective of the violations of export credit insurance policies and sales contracts by the exporter. This results in the assumption of the "exporter risk" by the credit insuring agency.

ICIA: *See* **International Credit Insurance Association**.

Indirect Exporter: A supplier of raw materials, intermediate goods, or component parts to an exporter.

Inflation Insurance: Insurance or guarantee cover that protects the exporter against a significant increase in the manufacturing costs of capital goods with a long lead time between contract signing and delivery. Also called *cost escalation insurance*.

Insurance: A contract of protection against loss in which the insurer undertakes to indemnify the policyholder in the event of a specified contingency or peril. An export credit insurer may offer insurance to both exporters and banks. Some export credit agencies refer to their insurance policies as guarantees.

Interest Rate Equalization: A program that provides to a commercial bank the difference between the interest rate payable by the exporter on the commercial bank's ECA-supported loan and the bank's cost of funds plus an agreed interest spread. Also called *interest subsidization* or *make-up*.

International Credit Insurance Association (ICIA): An association formed in 1928 to provide a forum for the exchange of ideas and information for private and governmental insurers that cover either domestic or export credit. The ICIA, based in London, has over 40 members from developing and industrial countries.

Investment Insurance: A form of political risk insurance protecting investors against specified risks related to their foreign direct investments. Coverage typically includes expropriation or nationalization without prompt and fair compensation and restrictions on repatriation of profits to the investor.

Letter of Credit: A document established by a buyer, evidencing a bank's commitment to pay an exporter up to a stated amount and within a stated time, based on drafts presented. This substitutes the bank's credit for the buyer's credit and is a major vehicle for financing foreign trade.

Level Payments: Amortization pattern in which the sum of principal and interest on each installment is the same. This implies increasing amounts of principal and decreasing amounts of interest as the date of final payment approaches.

Liability Limit: Maximum potential exposure of an export credit agency to pay claims under its insurance coverage for a single buyer or country or globally.

Line of Credit: A loan extended for a certain period of time to one obligor that may be used for multiple purchases for itself or other parties.

Local Costs: Expenses incurred for goods or services purchased from suppliers in the buyer's country. Export credit agencies do not usually finance or guarantee these costs but may do so up to a maximum of 15 percent of the export value.

London Club: The negotiating forum at which committees of commercial banks from creditor countries restructure debts owed to them by lenders in a country that is unable or unwilling to service its foreign debt. The London Club normally meets soon after the Paris Club. *See* **Paris Club**.

Long-Term: Repayment terms for exports of goods and services, generally from five years to ten years.

Loss: The amount that is subject to indemnification under a guarantee or insurance policy.

Management Fee: Fee charged by an export credit agency or commercial bank for services performed in the management of a project or syndicated financial arrangement. Sometimes called an *arrangement fee*.

Medium-Term: Repayment terms for exports of goods and services, generally from 181 or 365 days to five years. Under the OECD arrangement, medium term refers to repayment in two to five years.

Mixed Credit: Financial arrangement that includes a combination of export credit agency credit and concessional financing. Under OECD arrangement, if the subsidy element is greater than 25 percent, then the whole credit is considered aid. Also called *tied aid*.

Non-Acceptance Risk: Risk that a foreign buyer will fail to or refuse to accept goods shipped, provided the failure or refusal is not due to any fault of the insured exporter. Insurance against nonacceptance risk is commonly covered by export credit agencies as part of an export credit insurance policy covering commercial risk.

Non-Recourse Financing: An export credit extended to a foreign buyer in which the financing bank agrees not to seek recourse on the exporter in the event of nonpayment by the foreign buyer. This relieves the exporter of all risks of nonpayment, thereby increasing its own borrowing capacity.

OECD Arrangement: Agreement adopted in 1978 by members of the Paris-based Organization for Economic Cooperation and Development (OECD) to limit credit competition among the member governments in officially supported export credits. The guidelines cover cash payment requirements, minimum interest rates, maximum repayment periods, local costs, and procedures for negotiating any derogations from the Arrangement. The OECD arrangement superseded the OECD consensus. *See* **Consensus**.

Official Export Credit Agency: An export credit agency enjoying the financial participation or sponsorship of the national government, with the mandate of supporting the nation's exports.

Packing Credit: Pre-shipment advances made by a commercial bank to an exporter against firm export orders enabling the exporter to purchase, manufacture, and/or package goods for export.

Paris Club: Ad hoc meetings at which a country's debt owed to or guaranteed/insured by governments is restructured. A Paris Club agreement usually requires the debtor government to seek comparable relief from nongovernmental creditors. *See* **London Club**.

Part Period Cover: Insurance coverage for medium- and long-term transactions for which the export credit agency assumes risks associated with only a portion of the total credit terms.

Performance Bond: Bond issued by a financial institution on behalf of a supplier to assure the buyer that the supplier will perform according to the supply contract. The bond will compensate the buyer in the event that the supplier fails to perform. In some countries, insurance or guarantee coverage is available to protect the supplier or the bank/insurance company issuing the bond from the unjustified or capricious calling of the performance bond.

Political Risk: Insurance or guarantee cover that protects the exporter or financing bank from nonpayment by the buyer or borrower because of political events in the buyer's country or a third country through which either goods or payment must pass. The specific political events covered vary with different export credit coverage but generally include lack of foreign exchange; default of a sovereign entity; general moratorium on external debt; cancellation or nonrenewable of export or import licenses or import restrictions; delay in transfer of payments; war, civil war, and certain other events that prevent the exporter from performing under the supply contract or the buyer from making payment.

Post-Shipment Period: The period from date of shipment until final repayment of export credit by the foreign buyer.

Premium Rate: Cost of export credit insurance per unit, usually calculated on the gross invoice value for short-term sales or on the financed portion for medium-term sales.

Pre-Shipment Period: The period from the date of the contract signing to the date of shipment. Insurance or guarantee cover and/or financing may be extended.

Protracted Default Risk: A commercial risk typically defined by export credit agencies as payment unreceived six months or longer past maturity.

Reasonable Spread of Risk: A proportion of an exporter's short-term business deemed by an insurer to represent an acceptable range of risks with respect to both buyers and countries, rather than an adverse selection by the exporter against the insurer. Some export credit insurers require exporters to insure all exports; others only require a reasonable spread of risk; and some will insure specific buyers, transactions, or countries selected by the exporter. *See* **Adverse Selection**.

Recourse: The right of a bank or an export credit agency to demand payment from the maker of a draft or endorser of a note it has purchased, if the primary obligor fails to pay. Banks often finance exporters with recourse for transactions or portions of transactions that are not insured or guaranteed.

Recoveries: Amounts obtained by the export credit insurer from the foreign buyer following payment of a claim to an exporter or bank under insurance policies or guarantees. Any sums recovered are usually shared between the insurer and the exporter (or bank) in the same proportion as the percentage of cover and exporter (or bank) retention under the policy or guarantee. Also called *collections*.

Rediscount: A commercial bank's sale to an export credit agency, at a discount, of a borrower's obligation evidencing an export loan.

Reinsurance: Arrangement by which a portion of the premiums and risks insured by the export credit insurance agency are assumed by the government or other guardian authority or by private insurers. The government or other guardian authority usually provides reinsurance for political risks and losses in excess of the reserves of the export credit agency. Private reinsurers, sometimes as a group, undertake to reinsure a percentage of the risk (usually commercial only) on all or a specified proportion of the insurance business underwritten by an export credit insurance agency in return for a specific percentage of premium income.

Repayment Term: Schedule of payments to the exporter for goods purchased by a foreign buyer. The length of repayment terms generally reflect the type of product exported, the size of the transaction, the type of buyer, etc. *See* also **tenor**.

Rescheduling: Occurs when a debtor (public or private borrower) is unable to meet the original schedule of repayment called for in its loan agreement. Rather than repudiate or default, the debtor renegotiates the loan agreement, restructuring the payment schedule to provide additional term to meet its obligations.

Reserves: Provisions for losses based on historic or anticipated claims. Usually, reserves are calculated as a percentage of insurance outstanding and may also be segregated by type of coverage. Reserves are not considered capital of the export credit agency. *See* **Capital** and **Case Reserves**.

Retention: The percentage of the financed portion of a transaction on which the exporter or bank retains the commercial and/or political risk. *See* **Exporter Participation**.

Short-Term: Repayment terms generally of up to 180 days for exports of capital and equipment and machinery. Exceptionally, up to 365 days is considered short term. Berne Union guidelines for short-term credit insurance refer to repayment terms of up to two years depending on the product and the size of transaction.

Sovereign Buyer: A buyer that is owned by a national government and has the full faith and credit backing of that government when entering into sales or credit agreements.

Special Buyer Credit Limit: Maximum amount of credit set by the export credit agency that will be covered on a specified buyer when an exporter's shipments exceed the discretionary credit limit.

Specific Coverage: Insurance or guarantee cover for one particular transaction. An export credit agency may charge higher premiums for specific coverage than for whole turnover coverage because of the "selected risk" nature of specific coverage. *See* **Adverse Selection**.

Starting Point: The point in time when the amortization period of an export transaction begins. For most short-term transactions, the starting point is the date of shipment; for exports of capital equipment, the starting point may be the mid-point of deliveries or the date of installation; for long-term project finance, the starting point is usually the date of project completion. The due date of the first payment is usually six months after the starting point.

Stop Loss: Limits applied, usually in reinsurance contracts, on the amount of loss the primary insurer must absorb before filing a claim with the reinsurer. Many contracts of reinsurance provide stop loss limits per buyer, per country, and on total losses per annum.

Supplier Credit: Financial arrangement in which the supplier (exporter) extends credit to the buyer to finance the buyer's purchases. Normally the buyer pays a portion of the contract value in cash and issues a promissory note or accepts a draft to evidence the obligation to pay the remainder to the exporter. Also refers to commercial bank financing to an exporter for specific export sales made by the exporter on credit terms. Contrasts with **Buyer Credit**.

Tenor: Total repayment period. Also referred to as *term*.

Third Country Costs: Costs of procurement necessary for a project incurred in a country other than that in which either the project or the prime contractor is located. Some export credit agencies will cover such costs up to an amount equal to the cash payment.

Tied Aid: *See* **Mixed Credit**.

Transfer Risk: *See* **Conversion Risk**.

Waiting Period: The period following occurrence of a loss during which exporters or banks must wait before filing a claim with an export credit insurance agency.

Whole Turnover Policy: Insurance or guarantee cover for all or a negotiated portion of the export transactions of an exporter or bank, generally at a lower premium than for specific transactions due to the spread of risks. Also called a *global policy*.

Working Capital Loan: Credit used by an exporter to pay the expenses of producing goods for export, typically repaid out of export proceeds. Also called *pre-shipment loan* or *packing credit*.

Bibliography

Asian Development Bank. *Export Finance: Some Asian Examples*. Manila, Philippines: ADB, 1990.

Asociacion Latinoamericana de Organismos de Seguro de Credito a la Exportacion. *Bulletin No. 2*. Bogota, Columbia: ALASECE, 1996.

———. *Member Companies Directory 1996/1997*. Bogota, Colombia: ALASECE, 1996.

Bond, Daniel. *Country Risk Analysis at Ex-Im Bank and the Interagency Country Risk Assessment (ICRAS) Process*. Washington, DC: U.S. Eximbank, 1992.

———. *From Ordinal to Cardinal Measures of Country Risk*. Washington, DC: U.S. Eximbank, 1992.

Drummond, Paulo. *Recent Export Credit Market Developments*. Washington, DC: International Monetary Fund, 1997.

European Commission. "Communication Applying Articles 92 and 93 of the Treaty of Short-Term Export Credit Insurances." *Official Journal* C281. Brussels, Belgium: EC, 1997.

Export-Import Bank of India. *Export Credit Agencies Around the World: A Comparative Analysis*. Bombay, India: Eximbank of India, 1994.

Export-Import Bank of the United States. *Report to the U.S. Congress on Export Credit Competition*. Washington, DC: U.S. Eximbank, 1999.

First Washington Associates. *Export Credit Insurance Procedures Manual*. Arlington, VA: FWA, 1989.

———. *International Comparisons: Export Finance and Promotion Study*. Arlington, VA: FWA, 1991.

———. *Recommendations for a Model Export Finance System*. Arlington, VA: FWA, 1992.

———. *Special Report on International Competitiveness*. Arlington, VA: FWA, 1998.

———. *Special Report on the Role of Public and Private Companies in Export and Domestic Credit Insurance.* Arlington, VA: FWA, 1998.

———. *Study of Foreign Direct Investment Trends and Political Risk Investment Insurance Activity.* Arlington, VA: FWA, 1991.

———. *A Study of Institution Building for Post-Shipment Financing, Export Credit Insurance, and Guarantees to Banks in Developing Countries.* Arlington, VA: FWA, 1986.

———. *A Summary of Regional Trade Finance Programs.* Arlington, VA: FWA, 1996.

Gianturco, Delio. *Comprehensive Directory of the World's Export Credit Agencies.* Arlington, VA: FWA, 1991.

———. *The Trade and Export Finance Handbook.* London: Euromoney Publications/ First Washington Associates, 1994.

Global Business Communications. *Export Credit Reports.* Gillette, NJ: GBC, 1997.

Hamilton, Albert. *FWA Quarterly Newsletter.* Arlington, VA: First Washington Associates, 1992–2000.

Howell, Llewellyn D. *The Handbook of Country and Political Risk Analysis. 2d ed.* East Syracuse, NY: The PRS Group, 1998.

Insurance Institute of America. *The Global Environment of Insurance.* New York: McGraw Hill, 1999.

Inter-American Development Bank. *Evaluation Review on the Promotion and Financing of Exports.* Washington, DC: IDB, 1993.

International Association of Manufacturers. *Export Financing: A Key to U.S. Export Success.* Washington, DC: NAM, 1994.

International Credit Insurance Association. *1999/2000 Directory.* London, ICIA, 1999.

International Monetary Fund. *International Financial Statistics Yearbook, 2000.* Washington, DC: IMF, 2000.

———. *Official Financing for Developing Countries.* Washington, DC: IMF, 1998.

International Union of Credit and Investment Insurers. *The Berne Union: Export Credit Insurance, Overseas Investment Insurance.* London, Berne Union, 1988.

———. *The Berne Union 1999 Yearbook.* London, Berne Union, 1999.

International Union of Credit Insurers. *Collection of Histories of Members.* Paris, Berne Union, 1973.

Levitsky, Jacob. *Best Practices in Credit Guarantee Schemes.* Washington, DC: Inter-American Development Bank, 1995.

Organization for Economic Cooperation and Development. *Arrangement on Guidelines for Officially Supported Export Credits.* Paris: OECD Publications, 1998.

———. *The Export Credit Arrangement.* Paris: OECD Publications, 1998.

———. *Export Credit Financing Systems in OECD Member and Non-Member Countries.* Paris: OECD Publications, 1993 [Rev. 1999].

Proctor, Stephen D. *Maximizing Recovery of Commercial Debt Claims.* Washington, DC: U.S. Eximbank, 1988.

Rhee, Yung Whee. *Trade Finance in Developing Countries.* Washington, DC: The World Bank, 1989.

United Nations Conference on Trade and Development. *A Prototype Model of a Trade-Finance Facility in Developing Countries: An Export-Import Bank.* Geneva, Switzerland: UNCTAD, 1996.

———. *Review of Progress in Trade Finance Facilities of Developing Countries at the Interregional, Regional and Subregional Levels.* Geneva, Switzerland: UNCTAD, 1996.

———. *Trade and Development Report, 1997.* Geneva, Switzerland: UNCTAD, 1997.

———. *Trade Financing in Developing Countries: An Assessment and Evaluation of Existing Schemes and Future Requirements.* Geneva, Switzerland: UNCTAD, 1991.

United Nations Economic Commission for Europe. *Strengthening of Export Finance Support in Central and Eastern Europe.* Geneva, Switzerland: UN/ECE-ITC, 1996.

United States Eximbank. *Laws Relating to the Export-Import Bank of the United States.* Washington, DC: U.S. Eximbank, 1993.

———. *Report to the U.S. Congress on Export Credit Competition.* Washington, DC: U.S. Eximbank, 1999.

Venedikian, Harry M., and Warfield, Gerald A. *Global Trade Financing.* New York: John Wiley & Sons, 2000.

Watkins, Mary (ed.). *World Export Credit Guide, 1998–99.* London: Euromoney Publications/Bank of America, 1998.

World Bank. *Cofinancing Handbook: A Guide to Official Cofinancing Sources and Procedures.* Washington, DC: World Bank, 1995.

———. *Convention Establishing the Multilateral Investment Guarantee Agency.* Washington, DC: World Bank, 1985.

———. *Global Development Finance, 1998.* Washington, DC: World Bank, 1998.

———. *World Bank Lending for Export Development Funds.* Washington, DC: World Bank, 1983.

———. *World Development Indicators, 2000.* Washington, DC: World Bank, 2000.

World Trade Consultants, The Exporter Magazine, First Washington Associates. *Foreign Sources of Credit Information: A Global Guide.* New York: Trade Data Reports, 1989.

Index

About the Author

DELIO E. GIANTURCO is President of First Washington Associates, an international finance consulting firm active in 100 countries. Previously he was senior vice president, executive vice president, vice chairman and member of the board of directors for Export-Import Bank of the United States; governor in the Foreign Credit Insurance Association of New York; vice president, for the International Union of Credit and Investment Insurers (London), and senior adviser to the World Bank.